Edward Shippen

A Christmas at sea

Edward Shippen

A Christmas at sea

ISBN/EAN: 9783741193873

Manufactured in Europe, USA, Canada, Australia, Japa

Cover: Foto ©Andreas Hilbeck / pixelio.de

Manufactured and distributed by brebook publishing software (www.brebook.com)

Edward Shippen

A Christmas at sea

Why You Should Use Cleveland's Baking Powder

It is beyond question perfectly wholesome, being composed only of pure cream of tartar and soda, with enough flour added to keep the strength, no ammonia, no alum, no adulteration whatever.

It is the strongest. A rounded teaspoonful of Cleveland's Baking Powder does more and better work than a heaping teaspoonful of others. A large saving on a year's baking.

Cake and other articles of food keep moist and fresh and do not dry up as when made with baking powders containing ammonia or alum.

Housekeepers will be interested to know that Cleveland's Baking Powder is specified in the latest recipes of

MARION HARLAND,
Author Common Sense in the Household.

MARIA PARLOA,
Lecturer on Domestic Science.

Mrs. S. T. RORER,
Principal Philadelphia Cooking School.

Mrs. D. A. LINCOLN,
Author of Boston Cook Book.

Miss BEDFORD,
Late of Domestic Dept.,
Pratt Institute, Brooklyn.

Mrs. DEARBORN,
Principal Boston Cooking School.

Mrs. GILLETTE,
Author of "White House" Cook Book.

Miss HOPE,
Teacher in Public School Kitchen, Boston.

MARGARET WISTAR,
"Parlor and Kitchen," Philadelphia.

Mrs. GESINE LEMCKE,
Principal German-American Cooking
School, Brooklyn,

and many other prominent teachers of cookery.

ANOTHER VICTORY FOR CLEVELAND'S.

☞ On March 4th the contract for supplying the U. S. Army with baking powder was again awarded to the Cleveland Baking Powder Co. This makes the sixth consecutive order for Cleveland's Baking Powder from the government, and now the proposals specify that baking powder offered must be "in quality equal to Cleveland's." That is commendation that speaks volumes

"Gentle breath of yours my sails
Must fill, or else my project fails,
Which was to please."
Tempest.

"*Falstaff.* Have you provided me here half a dozen sufficient men?
Shallow. Marry have we, sir.
Falstaff. Let me see them, I beseech you.
Shallow. Where's the roll? where's the roll?
. . . . Let them appear as I call."
Shakspeare.

The "yarns" in this little volume are contributed by Rear-admiral Alexander Murray, who wrote Mr. Hawse's story, another officer of equally high rank, who remains anonymous, but, who wrote the "Admiral's Story," and the " Flag-officer's Story. Capt. C. H. Rockwell, who contributes the Captain's story, Ensign F. R. Brainard, who writes "An Amulet." Lt. T. B. M. Mason is the author of "The Secretary's Story." Pay-director Casper Schenck furnishes " Queen Annie " and the poem at the end of the book, while Capt. Charles King is the author of the Marine-officer's story. Medical Director Edward Shippen is the editor of the volume, the author of the introductions and condensation, and the Paymaster's and Assistant-surgeon's story. All the gentlemen named are officers of the navy, except Capt. King, who, as all the world knows, is an officer of the army.

A CHRISTMAS AT SEA.

A FINE taunt frigate, homeward bound from the East Indies, is in the Northeast Trades. The second dog-watch is far spent, and high in the eastern sky rides a lovely moon, across the face of which the soft billowy trade clouds are swiftly passing, as the strong breeze freshens with the night.

The ship carries all plain sail, with topmast studding-sails beside; which latter at times just lift enough to justify the ancient quartermaster at the "con" in reproachfully growling "No higher!" to which the seaman at the weather-wheel promptly answers, "No high!" and gives a spoke or two of weather-helm. "Werry well dice!" says the quartermaster, after a moment; while the officer of the deck, roused from a reverie of home by the incident, looks aloft, and then to windward, tells the petty officer to "keep her a good full," and once more steadies himself against the swifter of the mizzen rigging, and resumes the thread of pleasant thoughts.

Away forward, on both spar- and gun-decks, many groups of men, with folded arms, are pacing the planks in that restless, cat-like fashion which seamen have,—ten shuffling steps one way, and ten the other,—reminding one of the movements of animals in a menagerie. Others are gathered about some fiddler, or singer, or noted spinner of yarns; and now and then from these come snatches of chorus or bursts of hearty laughter. The officers, in pairs, are smoking on the gun-deck or pacing the lee-poop, or perhaps engaged in the after-dinner chat and chaff of the wardroom and steerage.

A listener near any of these groups, whether composed of officers or men, would find the one subject of conversation, song, or story to be *home*, with speculations innumerable upon the three months' news of which they are in arrears. The talk is mostly cheery and hopeful; but among those five hundred souls there must, of course, be some who have either dreary reminiscences or forebodings of bad news on arrival,—and these are the silent ones who, withdrawing from the crowd during this hour of recreation, brood in such dark nooks and quiet places as they can find,—while, far down in the sick-bay (silent at this hour, save for the creak of bulkheads and the plash of waters as the ship divides the seas), sways back and forth in his lonely cot one to whom all times will soon be alike, and whose mortal part will be consigned to the deep long before the welcome Land-ho! is heard on those decks. But these sad ones are few,—not enough even to leaven the mass of their shipmates,—and so the cheery talk and bustle goes on. Almost all have some plan, some joyful anticipation. The first lieutenant is to see his three-year-old boy for the first time. The third lieutenant is to be married. The paymaster is to resign and enter a great banking firm as soon as his accounts are settled. Others expect orders to the Naval School, the Observatory, or some hospital, if no "Coburgs" have cut them out during the period which has elapsed since the last mail was received on board.

Be sure that "Jack" has his plans, too, as well as his

master. With the exception of one Jerseyman, from Barnegat, who is to "buy into" a coaster and make a fortune, and of one or two Yankees, who are going fishing, not a soul of that ship's company is ever going to sea again. Many intend to purchase farms and plow the prairie; while those who doubt their ability as agriculturists are to work along shore as stevedores and riggers. The scapegrace landsman intends reform and a fresh start in life. The runaway boy is going home to his old mother, and means to ease his conscience by filling her lap with dollars; while the mainmast-man and the captain of the forecastle—grizzled tars—are going to the big house, as they call the Naval Asylum, to lay up in ordinary for the rest of their lives. The ship's cook, always a capitalist, is to open a canning establishment in Baltimore; while the barber, apt in a big ship to be another capitalist, has visions of a "tonsorial establishment" in a first-class city hotel, resplendent with plate-glass and mahogany, and profusely decorated with bottles of pink hair tonic.

Good resolutions swell most bosoms in that ship. The gun-deck of a homeward-bound man-of-war can be covered, tenfold, with the same material which is said to pave the lower regions. Nautical good intentions are, however, even less permanent than those formed on shore; and, in a few weeks, most of these busy planners will be shipped again, and outward-bound, leaving most of their hard-earned cash in the hands of whisky-sellers and sharpers, male and female, whose business in life is to prey upon "Jack," as gulls do upon herrings, or dolphins upon flying-fish.

It is a pity that the closing verse of the "Homeward-

Bound" song is not laid more to heart by those who follow the sea. It runs thus:

> " For when our money's gone and spent,
> And no more's to be found or lent,
> The landlord comes in with a frown,
> Says 'Jack, get up! let John sit down!'
> For he knows we're outward bound!
> He knows we're outward bound!"

But for the present, at least, the glamour of hope is upon all. Hope, long deferred, is seldom noisy, and the talk, though cheerful, is carried on in a subdued and earnest tone, the blended voices making a murmur throughout the crowded hull like the thrill and hum of bees in a hive.

Meanwhile the weary orderly at the cabin-door has been keeping a bright lookout upon the deck timepiece,—for his relief is near,—and eight o'clock having been duly reported, the officer of the deck suddenly breaks in upon the drowsy hum of voices with the sharp order, "Strike the bell eight! Call the watch!" The sound is not out of the bell ere the boatswain (who has been lingering for some time in the weather gangway, abreast the fore hatch), with a sharp, short chirrup, admonitory and preparatory,—answered immediately, in the same manner, by his mates,—proceeds to blow, in unison with them, a long-drawn winding "call," uniting the notes of the canary, the lark, and the cat-bird, and winding up abruptly with "All the watch!" His mates in turn sing out the same,—one bass voice deeper than another, until the last seems really to come from underneath the keel, "five fathoms deep." Now come up from the hatches, like ants from their holes, the watch

A CHRISTMAS AT SEA.

whose turn it is for duty. The lookouts and wheel are relieved, and the midshipmen go on with the muster.

Midst all this orderly bustle the lieutenant who has the first watch ascends from below with due dignity and deliberation, takes over the trumpet, receives the orders, course, and state of the weather from the officer he relieves, hails for a "bright lookout ahead," sees the braces taut, the rigging clear for running, admonishes the helmsman to keep her "full and bye," and settles matters generally for a comfortable fair-weather watch. Just then, too, emerges from the hatchway the form of the first lieutenant, who, having received the reports of the warrant-officers, and having interviewed the master-at-arms for about the twentieth time that day, is proceeding to make his last report to the commanding officer.

Captain Tangent is seated at the round table in the centre of the poop-cabin, the chart spread out before him under the swinging-lamp, waiting, not so much for the first lieutenant's report (the purport of which he knows beforehand) as for the appearance of the navigator with his work, showing the course and distance run since noon. The night orders are already written and lying upon the table, and the strong light shines upon a partly bald and grizzled head, a white but wrinkled forehead, in strong contrast with the deeply-bronzed cheeks, and an expression of countenance which shows that life has few illusions left for him, and that his temper has not improved with years.

Just now the captain is idly swinging his compasses round by one leg in the left hand, while, with a pencil in his right, he musingly makes an experimental dab at the supposed position on the chart. To him enters the first lieutenant, gives the stereotyped report, and asks if there are any orders. The official interview being then over, conversation begins.

"Fine night, Mr. Pawl. Glorious run these twenty-four hours! Pay for it by and by, though. Have it rough upon the coast at this time of year. Hope all are well at home. Christmas-eve, you know."

"Yes, sir. I was about to inquire if the men should have their Christmas as usual. They have made great preparations, and some of the messes will be well worth looking at."

"Certainly, Mr. Pawl, certainly! No work or drill! And let the band play at the men's dinner, and for dancing in the afternoon, if the weather permits."

This point settled, the first lieutenant then proceeds formally to request the captain to honor the wardroom mess with his company at dinner on the next day. The captain affects great surprise at the invitation, although for some days it has been an open secret that the admiral and captain were to be invited to dine out on Christmas-day; and neither of those veterans had made the slightest preparation to keep Christmas in their own quarters. In fact, their stewards had been furtively and busily engaged in assisting the wardroom steward in making boned fowls, pastry, and cunning devices in sweets, rivalling each other in the skill shown, after the manner of such gentry. Speedily recovering from his assumed surprise, the "skipper" politely assures Mr. Pawl that he "will have great pleasure," and the first lieutenant bows himself out. Thence, after a look at the weather, he descends to the gun-deck, and, after sending in his name by the orderly, is ushered into the admiral's cabin, where, with all due formality, the same invitation is extended and accepted.

"Christmas dinner, hey? Yes, pleasure! Ward-room mess must be better off for grub than I am, after a passage like this! In my time ward-room would be upon junk and duff!"

The gallant flag-officer is nearly sixty-two,—a smart officer still, and always a favorite in the service. Sanguine, courteous, amiable, hearty, he has a dark complexion, twinkling brown eyes, and hair, once jet-black, still so thick-set in his scalp that it stands up, as if in a state of surprise, in spite of all brushing or pomading. Powerful, square shoulders, deep chest, and rather long, nervous limbs gave the walk and bearing of an Indian, often making people suspect some trace of Cherokee blood in him.

As already remarked, everybody liked "Whisky," as he was frequently called behind his back,—nobody ever called him that to his face, not even his contemporaries. His father had been a noted Western distiller, of great wealth, and when his son entered the navy he was supplied with more money than fell to the lot of most young midshipmen. This, in the days when midshipmen's pay had not very much advanced from "nineteen and one," caused some envy, and he was at once nicknamed "Whisky," even by those who borrowed his money.

This was not seriously resented by him at the time; but by and by "Whisky" passed, and, being a bright fellow, passed high, and was ordered as master or navigator of a brig. One of his old messmates was ordered to the same vessel, and he, when all met at the time of reporting, at once hailed the master as "Whisky, old fellow!" But he was hauled up very short. "Shakings," said the master, "nicknames were all very well in the steerage, but now that I am of some account, I wish you to know that the man who calls me 'Whisky' must fight. You know that I don't mind you, old fellow, but I think it necessary to my dignity as an officer."

As it was well known that "Whisky" *would* fight,— indeed, had been a principal in more than one steerage duel, with ship's pistols,—he was never nicknamed to his face again, but resumed thenceforth his patronymic of Bluegrass.

The times have greatly changed since "Whisky" was a midshipman, when he and others would go on shore in the market-boat, pop at each other on the beach with ship's pistols, and with the stewards and the coxswain for witnesses, returning on board for breakfast little the worse for the operation. Or when the first lieutenant, "getting wind" of the proceeding, d—d them for young fools and quarantined them, while, three mornings afterward, he himself went out, and shot the doctor through the heart with his own hair-triggers.

But this is running away from our dear old flag-officer, whose genial nature renders the isolation enforced by his position rather irksome, and who is, in consequence, much given to entertaining the officers at his well-spread table. This it is easy for him to do, not only on account of comfortable private means, but because his children are long settled in life and off his hands; while his next in rank, the captain, has a large family still dependent upon him, is a trifle soured by the struggle of life, and avails himself of his solitary cabin to live quietly and economically, and seldom extends hospitality to any one.

And now to return to the dinner.

The invitations being accepted, a consultation of great import takes place between the first lieutenant and the caterer as to who is to be invited from the steerage, and how the table is to be made large enough for such an influx of guests. For, be it known, a wardroom table is, for the sake of compactness, not usually capable of comfortably seating more than the members of the mess. One of these is always on watch, so as to make a vacancy for a strange diner; while in port, when more strangers are apt to be present, some of the mess are sure to be absent on leave.

The caterer is a shrewd and wary veteran, who has, in the early part of the cruise, seen some willing and many unwilling members of the mess try their hands and fail,—for the most part ignominiously. Then he stepped in with plenary powers, and proving himself, by a reduction of expenses and an increase of comfort, eminently worthy, has ruled the mess ever since as a benevolent *pater familias*,—not denying his children reasonable comforts and indulgences, but for their own good limiting as far as possible things unwholesome both for stomach and purse. The important points referred to being settled, the caterer summons the steward. That important functionary appears at once, emerging from the pantry, his hands covered with flour and his whole person enveloped in a snow-white apron, being, in fact, in the act of " setting " the bread.

Domingo is a character, well known in the service.

I fear there are very few left like him. A native of Madeira, he had spent thirty years of his life in the navy; yet his English, though fluent enough, was hardly intelligible to a stranger, partly on account of his strong accent, but principally because it was largely made up of nautical idioms and expressions. Always respectful, though never servile; serving twenty masters well; thoroughly honest, trustworthy, and respectable; an economical marketer and excellent cook; with a reserve of force and dignity which enabled him to meet the vagaries of junior officers and easily control the crowd of negro wardroom boys; and with an experience and sharpness which confounded the devices of "galley-rangers," lucky was the mess which secured Domingo for a cruise.

Short and very square-built, close-shaven, with the blue-black beard showing through his olive, swarthy skin, with raucous, deep-toned voice, he was a type of his race. Neatly dressed at all times and in all weather, he was the one man on board ship who seemed always superior to the vicissitudes of sea-life. Bad indeed must the weather be when the wardroom table over which Domingo watched was not furnished forth at the appointed time; and low indeed must be the sea-stores when he had not some palatable dish ready to eke out the standing sea-fare. Such things are of less importance in these days of steam, short passages, and canned provisions; but in his early service they proved not only capability, but genius.

Remarkable as Domingo's English was, after a certain manner he was polyglot in tongue, and could hold his own in any market, from Singapore to San Francisco.

A CHRISTMAS AT SEA. 15

But especially did he pride himself upon speaking our language; and, during this very cruise, had taken great delight in teaching English, as he pronounced it, to some China boys who had filled vacancies among the wardroom servants, and was heard constantly to stir them up "becoz dey no bear a han' larnun Inglis."

Domingo assures the caterer that he is well forward in his preparations, and that he can turn in with the assurance that the reputation of the mess will be amply sustained, and that everything will go off well.

Christmas morning dawns with the same fine tradewind blowing, but a little more moderate than during the hours of darkness, and the ship tears on, with lurch and send, and a "bone in her mouth," flushing coveys of flying-fish from time to time, and keeping the spray diamonds dancing in the rising sun about her weather cat-head. The usual preliminary slopping, holy-stoning, squilgeeing, and swabbing is rather prolonged, in honor of the day, so that the ship may be pronounced thoroughly clean. During these processes the captains of the after-guard, the mastmen, quarter-gunners, and other petty officers exchange remarks of a pungent and even profane nature, little in keeping with the day, while the officer of the deck, with swinging trumpet, paddles fore and aft with bare feet and trousers tucked up; and the first lieutenant surveys the scene from the break of the poop, attired in pea-jacket and gum boots, and vaguely thinks he is aiding the work by sending for the boatswain and blowing him up, and by shouting for the foretopmen to bear a hand in the port gangway.

After breakfast the quarter-gunners put the last touch upon the guns, coil the lock-strings, and adjust the cap-squares, while the "black-listers" polish the bright-work until it won't stand another rub, and then the word is passed, after due preliminary of boatswain's call, for the crew to dress in clean mustering clothes, the usual work and exercises being dispensed with. At ten o'clock there is service on the gun-deck for those who choose to attend, —church being "rigged" by ranging chairs in a semi-circle for the officers, directly in front of which semi-lunar arrangement is the chaplain's desk, covered with bunting. The officers may be supposed to be in a state of grace, since the exhortations of the chaplain are directed point-blank in front of him. Here division-tube and hatch-coamings support capstan-bars, which form rather precarious and exceedingly uncomfortable seats for "Jack;" the latter, however, barring a vacant glance now and then, through the gun-deck ports, at the dancing blue-water to leeward, or an occasional general slide, during a lee lurch, pays all due attention to the chaplain's simple and touching story of the day. During the service the flag flies from the gaff, with the church pennant above it, for the benefit of the sea-birds and flying-fish we must suppose, for not a sail is in sight over all that grand expanse. Nothing, indeed, impresses one more with the immensity of the ocean than the fact that one may sail for days over a recognized and frequented route and yet never see a ship.

Soon after church is over seven bells strike, and there promptly appears at the fife-rail by the mainmast the fat and important-looking ship's cook with a great mess-pan full of the cooked ration for the day, in which, stuck upright, bristle and quiver a brightly-polished knife and spoon. The officer of the deck, tucking his trumpet

A CHRISTMAS AT SEA. 17

under his left arm, with a deliberate and supercilious manner which implies that the thing is a bore, proceeds to inspect and taste the appetizing mess. Being hungry after his forenoon watch, he really makes quite a hearty, if furtive meal. Then he pronounces it good,—the cook receives orders to "serve out," and, with his charger borne high, disappears down the fore hatch. A short pipe is heard, and then begins a clattering of mess-tins on the gun-deck as the mess-cooks lay the board,—in this case literally, for there is nothing but a tarpaulin between the pots and pans and the deck,—while a savory odor rises from the galley, and eddies aft upon the quarter-deck out of the big belly of the mainsail. At this time, too, appears the navigator, sextant in hand, with a swarm of "young gentlemen" similarly provided, and all intent upon the meridian altitude.

A lull of voices and a general suspension of movement now takes place for a few minutes, during which silence a tinkling of silver against glass is heard plainly upon the quarter-deck, transmitted up the hatches from the depths of the ward-room, and recognized by the initiated as the sound caused by the paymaster in preparing the "medicine" which he always takes at this hour, and they smile knowingly.

A few moments more, and the navigator lays his instrument upon the arm-chest, figures a little, and announces the latitude,—some of the young gentlemen being a few seconds behind him, for the look of the thing. "Orderly!" sings out the officer of the deck, "report to the captain 12 o'clock, latitude 19° 34′."

The orderly goes in, in one time and two motions, and reappears instantaneously with "Make it so, sir!"

"Strike the bell eight! Pipe to dinner! Heave the log!"

Alas for old-fashioned sailors! the last line of the old sea-rhyme no longer holds good. It used to run thus,—

> " Strike the bell eight!
> Heave the log!
> Pipe to dinner!
> And roll to grog!"

Since 1864 the marine drummer's roll to grog has ceased, and the main brace is now spliced in hot coffee, Jack's throat never experiencing the pleasant titillation of Old Rye save upon those rare occasions when it is served out by the surgeon in carefully measured and even niggardly doses as—medicine!

As the first lieutenant had said, some of the men's messes on the gun-deck are really well worth looking at. Their tins are scoured to a silvery polish, and their dishes are decked with curious paper devices from China and dried chrysanthemums of many colors from the Cape of Good Hope,—all carefully preserved under difficulties for this crowning feast of the cruise. Beside the standing ration of the day few there are without some dainty dish or succulent sea-pie, redolent of garlic and onions, while all have a well-cooked "duff," full of raisins. The petty officers' mess has even a roast pig,— rather large for stuffing and cooking whole, it is true, but not too much for the sturdy boatswain's and gunner's mates and swarthy, sun-browned quartermasters who surround it. Ever since the last port they have been furtively maintaining a small porker, and stuffing him with dainty bits, so that he has almost grown beyond the limits of galley ovens. All this time, too, they have been "working Tom Coxe's traverse" to keep the animal out of the first lieutenant's sight. Indeed, it is reported that he has made most of the passage in a division-tub, muzzled, to keep him from squealing. Perhaps Mr. Pawl has not chosen to be too keen-sighted in the matter of piggy, now that they are homeward bound, and the "Boston girls have got hold of the tow-rope," and so the animal has survived to fulfill his mission.

At the sergeant's mess, on the deck below, they have not only a table, let down from between the carlines, and camp-stools to sit upon, but also glass tumblers and knives and forks. Their dinner is served quite in form, and seasoned by genuine chutney, presented by the apothecary—an honored and influential member of the mess—in a disused leech jar; while another member, the yeoman, makes an offering for dessert of a pot of preserved Canton ginger, originally intended for his grandmother. Carried away by the spirit of the festive occasion, he determines to present her instead with a cheap Canton work-box, already so warped by change of climate that it will neither open nor shut.

Dinner over, the men lounge and smoke, sing, dance, and skylark, while the band gives them their own favorite airs. Some of them take out their ditty-bags, and take a sailor's comfort in patching and turning and mending, like thrifty housewives, although public opinion rather discourages anything of the kind on such a holiday, and when homeward bound, as savoring of meanness. It is past comprehension how an old sailor will deny himself tobacco and submit himself to reprimand for wearing patched and shabby clothing, and he may save a few more dollars to go into the maw of the land-shark predestined to meet him in Water Street or Cherry Street, and lead him off like a sheep to be shorn.

Meanwhile the fair trade lasts well. Hardly a brace is touched; the temperature is perfect, and the ship bowls along with just enough of send, and lurch, and stagger to make one realize that she is going her best pace, and that every hour knocks off eleven knots from the distance home. The band has ceased to play, but no evening quarters disturb the holiday, which those who have no watch on deck pass as best pleases them. In the port gangway the foretopmen are playing "bull in a ring," in the other the maintopmen are singing of a frigate, "a frigate of fame, which in the East Indies she bore a great name." Listen to them for an instant:

> "Now all in one moment this work must be done.
> It's 'all hands reef topsails and tack ship in one;'
> It's 'lay aloft topmen,' as the hel-lum goes down,
> 'Trice up and lay out and take two reefs in one.'"

A worthy set of solemn and grizzled forecastlemen are exchanging reminiscences as to whether the "Ironsides" or the "Pelter" first opened fire at Fort Fisher; and how they got the "Teaser's" anchor when she slipped after a blockade-runner off Mobile in '63; with occasional diversions to settle whether it was Tom Scott or Bill Scott who kept a sailor boarding-house in Cherry Street in 1850, and whether the name of the captain of the forecastle of the "Ripsnorter," round the Horn in '49, was Henry Jones or Eliphalet Robinson. Upon the gratings about the stern of the launch is gathered a group of sentimental and imaginative youths, who are listening with open ears and mouths to one of those interminable yarns or narratives so dear to the nautical mind.... "'Now, says the Prin-cess,' says she, 'this here beats the speckled Jews!' And she got right up and called for her elephant, and went off mad; and all her harpoon-guard went with her."

So passes the time on deck. In the wardroom the event of the afternoon is the throwing for choice of certain lots of plated ware, books of reference, and a fine painting of the ship,—owned in common by the mess, and valuable intrinsically, as well as souvenirs of the cruise. Before six all the officers are dressed and ready for dinner, and, on the stroke of the bell, the fife and drums play "Roast Beef;" the first lieutenant goes for the admiral, and the caterer for the captain, who are, with naval punctuality, all ready; and these high officials are escorted below in due state. Upon entering the wardroom they are received by the mess, all standing and executing a general chassez across. "Good-evening" and remarks upon the weather then succeed, as if the visitors had just come on board from some neighboring island and no one had seen or heard of them for months.

By a nautical fiction the flag-officer is supposed to be only a passenger on board the flag-ship,—having his headquarters and establishment there, but not commanding her any more than any other vessels of his command: so the intercourse between himself and the captain need be only formal and official, he telling the captain where he wishes to go, and the latter taking him to his destination. Thus these two gentlemen meet in the wardroom as in the house of a mutual friend; and now remarks upon the weather, and upon the prospects for a good passage, are exchanged by them. The sea-stores of the steerage have long since run low, and there is no danger of the invited guests from the mess not knowing when dinner is ready, although no one is sent for them. Messieurs Mid, Fid, Forward, and Chuckles therefore slide quietly in and skirmish in the rear, while the high dignitaries are exchanging compliments and meteorological remarks.

The proper moment having now arrived, the company go to dinner. The admiral is seated in the middle of the table, with the captain opposite to him. The rest take their accustomed places, with a midshipman sandwiched in here and there. The chaplain says grace,—rather longer than usual, as befits an occasion of high festivity, —at the conclusion of which the bandmaster, who has been peering down the hatch to observe the exact moment, waves his baton (an octave flute), and the band on the half-deck crashes into the "March in Norma," with entirely too much trombone. Then the wardroom boys advance from a dim and gloomy space in the rear, bearing dishes, and showing inches of black wrist, in sharp contrast with the white cotton gloves some sizes too small for them.

Soup is served, and consumed in silence; and then the sherry glasses are filled; apropos of which act the admiral—who is, as usual, in a gracious mood—relates a little story of Peter Domecq, Xeres, and the year 1826. This the captain straitway supplements by a reminiscence of Messina, anno 1838, and of some Bronté wine, "which no one could tell, begad! from March's best navy Madeira."

The appositeness of the latter anecdote is not apparent, but it is received with great appearance of interest, and, the ice being broken, conversation begins. Members of the mess ask when the captain thinks he will get in. Non-committal answer, and a reference to the superior wisdom of the admiral. Admiral thinks it uncertain, especially at this time of year; and so that subject seems exhausted at its very inception, which is a pity, for mess jokes and topics are of course excluded; and this one seemed thoroughly conservative and safe.

Another member of the mess cheerfully remarks that "they are having their health drank at many a dinner at home to-night." The captain, still non-committal, remarks that "that's as may be;" after which comes a prolonged silence, and a determined attack upon the dinner, during which Mr. Gasket, the third lieutenant (who had been suspended, not long before, for carrying away a top-mast studding-sail boom), remarks *sotto voce*, to his next neighbor, that "the skipper is as cross as a bear with a sore head;" at which, in the midst of the silence, his neighbor laughs out, but immediately puts on preternatural solemnity as all eyes are turned in his direction. In fact, the dinner promises to be very stiff, and the promoters of the festivity are beginning to feel very blue, when the caterer comes to the rescue by ordering champagne, which appears properly cooled in a cunning mixture devised by the assistant surgeon. There are only six bottles of it left, and the members of the mess have been privately admonished to touch it lightly; while the steward, in serving it, passes over one of the midshipmen altogether, to his great disgust.

With the appearance of the wine the condition of affairs rapidly improves; and, in a few minutes, the captain, with a glance at the admiral, vouchsafes the remark that he "hopes to get in about the twelfth." The admiral adds, condescendingly, " tenth to fifteenth." The champagne is passed round again, and neither the first lieutenant nor the caterer take any this time, while Domingo deliberately passes over the chaplain and another midshipman. Conversation soon becomes general and easy, and the elaborate dessert is consumed amidst universal chat and hilarity, the midshipmen, meantime, making play at the decanters, as they know their time is short.

By and by eight o'clock lights are reported out by the master-at-arms at the wardroom door.

This functionary is a character. A sort of Ishmael, he has no sympathy with any soul on board. He does, to be sure, slightly defer to the first lieutenant, as his proper superior, but really, and at heart, he pities him for his weaknesses. He reports "ten o'clock lights out," "John Brown is dead," "Peter Smith is in double irons," or the "berth-deck's on fire" in the same tone, and with the same wooden face and manner.

As the master-at-arms disappears (having shown by his looks that he deeply disapproves of any such unbending and frivolity), the bustle of relieving the watch is faintly heard, and the guests from the steerage discreetly rise and excuse themselves. Claret and Madeira are now placed upon the table by the steward, who stations himself behind the caterer's chair, and glows with the consciousness of duty well performed, as well as with the heat of the pantry, from which he has emerged.

As both admiral and captain like a cigar, special permission for smoking below is granted, for this occasion only, and trays of Manillas, the only cigars possible in that ship, are placed upon the table.

The two important guests are by this time beaming with good nature, and—*plenum vini ciboque*—light their cigars, while the admiral says, " If you don't mind, gentlemen, I will tell you a little story of a Christmas night long ago, of which I am reminded forcibly by contrast with the pleasant weather we are now enjoying. It has a spice of the supernatural about it, and is, in fact, the only approach to communication with the spirits which ever occurred to me. This is the more remarkable, as I paid due heed to their communications on that occasion; and I have been given to understand by latter-day professors that they seldom leave those who do so. Well, on this occasion I certainly had a warning from a mysterious voice; and, although by no means superstitious, am still inclined to think that

> ' There are more things in heaven and earth, Horatio,
> Than are dreamt of in your philosophy.'

In the year 18— I found myself attached as a watch-officer to the ' V——,' one of the ships belonging to a squadron stationed on the west coast of Africa, cruising there for the suppression of the infamous slave-trade. This ' V——' was a stanch, old-fashioned, deep-waisted sloop-of-war of nearly eight hundred tons burden, carrying twenty guns, with a complement of more than two hundred souls in her ship's company. She had been built years previously, during the régime of the ' Navy Commissioners,' but at this time, from the many repairs that had been made upon her hull, there was scarce a stick of the original timber remaining, although her model had been sacredly preserved

'Through all the changes of the changing years.'

There was a report current in naval circles relative to the modeling of this vessel and of her sister-ships,—for we had six of these naval beauties in our service,—that the said Navy Commissioners, when they had assembled together for the purpose of examining plans and deciding upon the model by which the vessels should be constructed, had selected that one from which they were afterwards built, by first reducing their length of keel, as on the original plan, *from one hundred and sixty* to *one hundred and thirty feet*, and this reduction in their length was made by cutting those thirty feet *square off from the after part of the model*. As the 'V———' had very full quarters, and anything but a clear run, this current report was in all probability correct.

Notwithstanding this reduction of length the 'V———' was a comfortable 'old tub,' that could run along from six to eight knots under favorable conditions of wind and sea, while with a quartering gale she could go ten.

Our captain was a tall, thin, nervous old gentleman, who had not seen much service afloat, and consequently was not a practical seaman. He had grave doubts as to the stability of any ship of war when under canvas, and was particularly fearful that this one which he commanded would either be capsized during some squall, or else wrecked by running upon rocks or shoals. These dangers to navigation, although not laid down upon our charts, nevertheless existed, in his imagination, on every mile of the broad Atlantic. It was his standing order that the officers of the deck should reduce sail whenever in their opinion it was necessary to do so, reporting the facts afterwards. But no one, not even the first lieutenant, could make sail; the captain, and the captain only, could order sail to be made after it had once been taken off the ship. In consequence of this order the officers were very chary in reducing sail, and did so only when in their opinion it was absolutely necessary.

In the wardroom we had six line-officers and four idlers as messmates. The former were old 'sea-dogs,' each one of whom, from long experience, knew how to handle a ship under any and every occurring circumstance, and the latter were jolly fellows, who always kept the first watch when at sea under the starboard side of the top-gallant forecastle, there smoking their pipes and spinning their yarns.

After a very warm day, hot even for the African coast, the sun had disappeared behind the horizon, leaving a breeze which seemed to us smokers, who were forward enjoying our pipes, to be deliciously cool; then, as star after star appeared, there was every promise of a lovely night. Eight bells were struck, and the watch was called, as I went aft to relieve the officer of the deck, who, after passing me the orders, the sail set, and the courses to be steered, started forward for my vacated seat, there to have a whiff from his pipe, and to enjoy the lovely night ere turning in. I walked around the deck, examined the weather-head braces, the trim of the yards, and the set of the sails. After satisfying myself on each of these points I looked at the compass, and went upon the poop to scan the horizon as to the present and future prospects of the weather. Everything appearing to be fair, I settled myself into a steady walk, which was to continue, as I supposed, during the four hours I was to be the guardian of the ship and her crew. The weather at this time was delightful, the stars were shining with remarkable brilliancy; indeed, they were so very brilliant that each particular star appeared to be *the star* that outshone all the others, and to be *the one* that singly and alone gave all the light illuminating the heavens.

Not a cloud could be seen in any direction; there was nought to mar the brightness of the sky above, and the waters beneath were scarcely ruffled by the gentle breeze that silently moved our ship over their surface. Under royals and flying-jib, with the wind abeam, our ship sailed over this 'summer sea' almost as noiselessly and gracefully as an albatross skimming the ocean's crest.

It was the custom on board, owing to the excessive heat during the daytime, to grant the ship's company the privilege of singing and smoking until nine o'clock, which is an hour later than the time usually allowed on board ships of war when at sea. This hour having arrived, orders were given to pipe down, and for the watch to lie aft on the quarter-deck, and stow themselves on the weather side, between the guns; the log was hove and the lights reported out; five knots was the speed of the ship. Everything then became quiet about the decks; and there was at this time no appearance, in any quarter, of any change either in wind or weather.

The night was so very beautiful, and the stars so very bright, that I could not refrain from repeating to myself,—

THE ADMIRAL'S STORY.

> 'If yon bright stars which gem the night
> Be each a blissful dwelling-place,
> Where kindred spirits reunite
> And live to meet the loved of this—'

Thus far only had I spoken, when a voice whispered gently in my ear,—

'*You had better shorten sail.*'

The words were spoken very distinctly, and I turned around expecting to see the speaker; but I was alone at the break of the poop, and there was no one near me. As I was certain that I had heard the words, it was some time before I could satisfy myself that I might have been mistaken, for if I was not, *from whence could the voice have proceeded?* Resuming my walk and cogitating over the matter, the time passed quickly, and four bells were reported and struck; then I gave the usual orders to—

'Relieve the lookouts! Heave the log! Muster the watch! Report the ten o'clock lights out!'

The log again gave five knots as the speed, and there was still no change of wind or of weather. After this I took a stroll around the deck, felt of the weather-head braces, and looked at the yards; finding everything 'taut and trim,' I went upon the poop, and stood at the starboard quarter scanning the horizon, *and while in this position looking to windward*, the same gentle voice again whispered in my ear,—

'*You had better shorten sail.*'

This time there was no mistake, and I looked around, as I had upon the previous occasion, expecting to see the speaker, but there was no one in sight who could possibly have spoken; indeed, the only person on the

poop besides myself was the lookout, stationed at the
'life-buoy' on the port quarter, and he was standing,
facing to leeward, watching the phosphorescence of the
sea, utterly oblivious of everything save of his own
thoughts.

He certainly was not the mysterious speaker. Who
was? I am not easily startled, nor am I superstitious,
but is it to be wondered at that I felt, to say the least,
queerly, knowing mysterious beings were around who
could make themselves heard, yet could neither be seen
nor felt? Then I argued to myself, this whisperer is
evidently friendly, as accidents do not result from being
under short sail, while many terrible ones have resulted
from carrying too much. Reasoning thus, although the
stars were still as brilliantly shining, the wind as gently
blowing, and the ship as quietly sailing as when my
watch commenced, and although there was not a cloud
to be seen, I gave orders,—

'Furl the royals and stow the flying-jib;' then
ordered the watch to remain on their feet, not to lie
down any more, but to see and keep everything clear for
shortening sail; after this I went forward on the top-
gallant forecastle, looking at the horizon from all points
of view there; but nothing could be seen indicating a
change.

As I passed down the forecastle-ladder on my way
aft, each one of the idlers seated forward greeted me
with,—

'Halloo, Bluegrass, what's the matter?'

'Why are you taking in sail?'

'Are there any squalls brewing?'

As I could give these questioners no good reasons

for my action, I preserved a dignified silence and continued on my way, resuming my walk upon the poop, where, in less than five minutes' time and while I was in the act of walking the deck, that same mysterious voice whispered once more,—

'*You had better shorten sail.*'

This was the third time of the warning, and as at the previous time, so now, there was no one in sight or near who could have spoken. *I was alone!*

Hesitating no longer, I made every preparation for stripping the ship of her canvas, but before giving the final orders to do so, examined again the horizon to windward, and there in the far distance perceived a misty appearance, as of an Indian summer haze, and I also thought I could hear a sound like unto that made by wind as it soughs through a forest in winter-time. Ordering the quartermaster to make a judicious luff and lift the weather-leaches of the topgallant-sails, I took them in, and was about ordering them furled when there came a sound, a rushing sound, increasing instantly to a roaring like unto that made by Niagara's mighty fall, and with time only to order, 'Hard up the helm! Let go the main-sheet! Let go the lee topsail-sheets! Let go the topsail-halliards!' when a furious blast struck the ship, forcing her over under its mighty power, until the muzzles of our lee guns were buried in the water, while at the same time a dense mass of spray or mist was driven over the rail with a force that blinded every one. As the ship herself was almost thrown on her beam-ends by the first puff of the squall, so all on deck were thrown down, and found themselves struggling in the lee-scuppers. For a few moments, what with the howling of the wind, the slapping of canvas, and the impossibility of standing upright, it appeared to me doubtful whether or no I should be able to save either the sails or the spars; but our stanch old ship paid off slowly and surely, and as the force of the wind was brought abaft the beam the crew picked themselves up and worked with a will in carrying out my orders.

At length discipline, combined with the preparations that I had made, enabled me to triumph over the fury of the squall, and by the time the ship was before the wind the topsails had been clewed up and the mainsail hauled snugly up to the yard; then close-reefing the topsails, I set the fore and main and furled the mizzen, then sent the topgallant and royal yards on deck. Looking around to see what damage had been done, I found the foresail and jib were split, and the fore-topgallant-sail blown away from the jack-stay; there were also a few bruised limbs among those who had been pitched to leeward. All the smokers forward lost their pipes and tobacco, and received a thorough drenching, while the watch-officers who had '*turned in*,' being on the weather side of the ship, were all '*turned out*' in a most unceremonious manner, finding themselves suddenly sprawling on the deck in their state-rooms.

Everything was 'to rights' at last, the ship running before the wind, when as suddenly as the squall had begun, so as suddenly it ceased, passing away in a cloud of mist, and disappearing in the distance to leeward, leaving nothing to mark its pathway save our good ship stripped of her canvas and lying almost motionless on the water. I went to the cabin to report, and found the

captain standing at the door, looking very pale and very miserable. After giving him the details of the squall and of my actions in regard to the ship, he remarked,—
'That was a terrific squall, Mr. Bluegrass.'
'Yes, sir,' I answered, 'it was quite heavy. I think it must have been a "*white squall*"; but it is all over now; it has passed ahead; and as the weather is as it was previous to its advent, with every indication of continuing fair, shall I make sail?'

'*Make sail, sir!!*' he answered, with indignation expressed in his tones,—'*make sail, sir!!! No, sir!!!*' Thus the interview ended, and sail was not made on the ship in a hurry.

White squalls, so called, are of very rare occurrence. No seafaring person of my acquaintance has ever experienced one. Even with my fifty years of service, this was the first and last I have ever met. Showing, as they do, few or no signs of their approach, and traveling with great velocity, they are particularly dangerous, and woe betide that unfortunate vessel overtaken by one, if unprepared to meet it, for she must either be dismasted at the first fury of the blast, or else forced over by its mighty power, be capsized, and

'In the deep bosom of the ocean buried.'

From the time when I discovered the far-distant mist that heralded the approach of this one until the time when it had passed away not an hour elapsed, and it left us with the stars as brightly shining, the wind as gently blowing, and the sea almost as smooth as it had been before its coming.

As I have stated, sail was not made again on the

'V——' in a *hurry*, for, during the space of four days and nights, she remained under the short sail that I had reduced her to, the captain not permitting any more to be made, being fearful lest another white squall might be 'bottled up' somewhere in the universe, only to be let loose upon his devoted head. At last, to the surprise of every one, sail was ordered to be made, and in due time we arrived safely at Porto Prayo, where, finding the commander-in-chief, our captain reported

'The dangers he had passed.'

In conclusion, I ask, whence came that mysterious voice, but for whose repeated warnings I should not in all probability have discovered the approach of that squall in time to prevent at least serious damage to the ship, or perhaps her loss altogether? I ascribe the voice and those warning words to that

'Sweet little cherub
That sits up aloft,
And looks out for the life of
Poor Jack.'"

The flag-officer having finished his story, said, "I have spun rather a long yarn, for me, but Christmas times always bring that night vividly before me. I feel now that I have a right to call upon Captain Tangent to give us a reminiscence of his own."

"What!" says the captain. "Why, sir! I never told a yarn in the whole course of my life."

And, indeed, no one had ever known the "skipper" to do so in the whole of a long cruise, at least, he being perhaps the most matter-of-fact and taciturn person on board, however sensible and reliable.

THE CAPTAIN'S STORY.

When he heard the captain thus called upon, Mr. Gasket, the third lieutenant, at his end of the table, in a voice only audible to those immediately around him, remarked " Umph! *his* reminiscences consist of different 'horsings' of officers of the deck, and quarantining of midshipmen for not having their journals written up." Great indeed, then, was the astonishment of the company when the captain, with a preliminary glass of Madeira, actually began a story.

"If you like," he said, "I'll give you a yarn of the old times, about a very well-known man to old officers, —Captain Thomas Tempest. It was a dark gloomy morning in the month of March, 1844. Off the Battery in the harbor of New York, lay the sloop-of-war *Champlain*, about to sail for the West Indies and the Spanish Main. The wind was raw and fresh from the N. N. W. The sky was overcast, and there was a feeling of snow in the air. The chain had been hove short, the topsails were set, and the courses, top-gallant sails, jib and spanker were loose, and ready for making sail. The ship had been put under 'sailing orders' for midnight, the day previous, which meant that everyone should be on board at that time. Before lifting the anchor, the captain directed the first lieutenant to beat to quarters, to see if every officer and man was on board and at his station.

The lively music of the drum and fife started everyone hurrying to his station, and the men were rapidly mustered, and the division officers passed aft to report all accounted for to the executive officer.

All reported but one officer. The waist division

seemed to have its full complement of men, but Lieutenant Singleton, the officer in charge, was not at his quarters.

'Corporal of the Guard,' sang out Mr. Draper, the first lieutenant, 'go below, and see if you can find Mr. Singleton.' The corporal soon returned, saluted, and reported.

'Mr. Singleton is nowhere below, sir.' Hurried inquiries revealed the fact that no one had seen the lieutenant, and so the executive reported to the captain.

'Officers and men all accounted for, sir, except Lieutenant Singleton, who is not on board the ship.'

Captain Tempest was a 'Tartar.' Fierce and rigid in his ideas of discipline, he was stern and exacting, and inflicted punishment with an unsparing hand when he deemed it necessary. He had given orders on the preceding day that all the officers should be on board by midnight, and here was one missing, and his orders had been disregarded.

'Were all the officers informed of the fact that the ship was under sailing orders at midnight?' he sternly asked the first lieutenant.

'They were, sir,' answered that officer.

'Has the Navy Yard boat shoved off yet?' inquired the captain.

'No, sir.'

'Detain her, sir, I have a letter to send,' and retiring to his cabin he wrote the following despatch to the Honorable Secretary of the Navy.

U. S. SHIP 'CHAMPLAIN,'
NEW YORK HARBOR, March 14, 1844.

SIR:—Lieutenant Gustavus Singleton of this ship went on shore yesterday with directions to return on board by midnight. He failed to do so, in direct violation of my orders.

I trust that the Honorable Secretary will see that suitable punishment is inflicted upon this delinquent. I shall sail without him.

Very Respectfully,

THOMAS TEMPEST, Captain Commanding.

The Honorable J. R. MASON, Secretary of the Navy.

'Send this letter by the Navy Yard boat. Get under way, sir,' said the captain.

On the preceding day, Lieutenant Singleton had gone on shore to make a few purchases, and to have a ramble through the streets, intending to return on board the *Champlain* in the sunset boat. He had finished his business, and was sauntering slowly down Broadway, when he saw a carriage drawn by a pair of spirited horses, which were evidently unmanageable, come dashing up the street towards him. Without an instant's hesitation he sprang at the heads of the frightened animals, and caught the one nearest him by the bridle. The velocity of the horses dragged him for some distance, but his weight finally threw the horse, which fell heavily upon the young man. The struggling animals were quickly secured, and the lieutenant was borne insensible into a drug store.

The occupants of the carriage were two ladies, evidently mother and daughter. They were much frightened, but unhurt, and, procuring another carriage, were driven rapidly away, without seeming to know just how their vehicle had been stopped, or what had happened.

Lieutenant Singleton fell into good hands. His wounded head was plastered and bandaged, and regaining consciousness, he soon fell asleep under the influence of opiates, and slept until morning.

When he awoke, he shouted:

'Hello! where am I?'

'In the surgery of Hobson's drug store,' said an attendant coming forward.

'How came I here, and what is the matter with me?' he asked.

The case was explained to him, and then he remembered who he was, and about the ship.

'What time is it?' he said, anxiously.

'Nearly eight o'clock in the morning,' was the answer.

'Get a carriage instantly,' he cried. 'My ship will sail without me.'

So he drove rapidly to the Battery, and saw the *Champlain*, under all sail, going down the harbor.

He chartered a tug and started in chase, and finally caught the ship off the Romer, and was assisted on board.

He was a sorry sight. His head was bandaged, his left arm was in a sling, and his clothing was soiled and torn.

Captain Tempest, rigid, wrathful and neat in his undress uniform, stood upon the quarter deck as Mr. Singleton came on board. The latter was weak, and tottered as he reached the deck.

The Captain blazed at once.

'Sir, you are a disgrace to the service. You are evidently intoxicated, and have probably been in some drunken brawl. Go below, sir, and consider yourself under arrest. Deliver your sword to the First Lieutenant, and confine yourself to the quarters that will be assigned you.'

'Captain,' faltered Singleton, 'an unfortunate accident——'

'Silence, sir!' thundered the Captain; obey the order I have given you instantly.'

Singleton turned to go below, but the excitement had been too much for him, and he fell fainting to the deck, and was carried to his quarters.

Captain Thomas Tempest, although a rigid disciplinarian, was a fine officer. He had a gallant record, and stood very high with his superiors. His subordinates respected his abilities, but would prefer to serve in some other ship. His fierce temper and unyielding disposition made him many enemies, but any duty entrusted to him was certain to be performed well, and as he was not afraid of responsibility, his reputation was good.

The surgeon promptly placed Lieutenant Singleton upon the sick list, and reported him as suffering from 'contusion of the head, lacerated left arm, and many bruises.'

Captain Tempest sent for the surgeon.

'Doctor, how was this officer injured?' he inquired.

'I am unable to find out, sir,' said the surgeon. 'He is feverish and slightly delirious.'

'These young men have very bad habits,' said the captain. 'He has undoubtedly been on a spree, and has been engaged in a disgraceful brawl. I shall make an example of him. He was drunk when he came on board.'

The doctor was a man of experience and made no answer. He kept his counsel and retired.

The *Champlain* made good speed southward. The gloomy weather was soon left behind, and the balmy breezes and azure skies of the ocean beyond the Gulf Stream made all on board soon forget the March blasts and the chilling clouds of the coast. Heavy clothing was put away, and a summer brightness filled the air. The trade winds were met well north, and the noble ship, with every sail drawing, stood up gallantly to her work, and on the tenth day after leaving New York, swept majestically into the harbor of St. Thomas, and saluted the flag officer in command of the squadron with thirteen guns.

Captain Tempest went on board the Flag-Ship in full uniform, to report to the Commander in Chief. An officer's guard was paraded on the quarter deck, which presented arms as he came over the side, and he was conducted to the cabin with much ceremony, where he was received by the kind-hearted old Flag-Officer. After presenting his report of the passage out, the Captain handed in a paper giving in detail the circumstances of the case of Lieutenant Singleton.

The Commander in Chief had grown old in his country's service. His venerable head was crowned with a glory of grey hair, and a more honorable, upright man, never wore the Naval uniform. He was always just, but dearly loved mercy. He remembered that he had once been young, and that youth is a season of high spirits and generous impulses. The case, by Captain Tempest's report, was a grave one, but the venerable Officer desired to sift the matter thoroughly before taking action. 'Captain,' said he, 'this is a very serious report. What is the reputation of this officer?'

'He has never sailed with me before sir, and has recently joined my ship. There was no cause of complaint against him until this occasion, when he deliberately disobeyed my orders, came on board in a disreputable condition, and was so drunk that he fell insensible on the deck before me, as the report recites. These occurrences are becoming too common, and I trust you will bring him to trial by a court martial.'

Captain Tempest really believed that his statements were true. The rigid condition of his mind and temper led him to suppose that the requirements of justice and discipline could not be satisfied, unless this young officer was severely punished; and so, by every argument in his power he endeavored to persuade the flag officer to order a court martial.

Lieutenant Singleton recovered his bodily health under the care of the surgeon, but his mind cherished deep resentment for the unjust treatment that he was subjected to. He brooded over his troubles, and sometimes felt impelled to resign his commission and leave a service where arrogance could inflict such hurtful blows, and where his proud spirit could be so wounded. He kept his counsel strictly, made no confidants, and nourished his wrongs in his own heart, but gave no sign of what he suffered.

He was furnished a copy of the captain's report to the flag-officer, and was given an opportunity of making any explanation that he saw proper.

Smarting under a sense of wrong, he contented himself with a brief answer, disclaiming any disobedience of orders, accounting for his appearance by an accident that temporarily disabled him, and emphatically denying any intoxication.

When this communication, which was curt and not particularly respectful, reached the commander-in-chief, that officer read it several times, and reluctantly convened a general court-martial to try Lieutenant Singleton.

On the succeeding week a small blue ball was run up to the mizzen royal masthead, a gun was fired, the stops were broken, and the Union jack floating on the breeze showed that a naval general court-martial was in session on board the flag-ship. It was composed of nine officers, all senior to the accused, and they assembled in full uniform to perform their grave and important duties.

At a long table in the cabin the court sat. The president, in this case the captain of the flag-ship, was at its head. On his right sat the officer next in rank, the second on his left, the third on the right, and so on. At the foot of the table sat the judge advocate, a captain of marines. Before each member was placed writing materials, and the various law books in use, were on the table for reference if necessary. At a smaller table, on the right of the judge advocate sat the accused.

The court was organized, and the first officer to be tried was asked if he objected to any member of the court, sitting on his trial.

Lieutenant Singleton had no objection to any member present, and the president of the court administered the oath to the judge advocate, and then the members standing in a circle, each with his ungloved right hand resting on the Bible, were sworn to ' well and truly try, without prejudice or partiality, the case now before the court.' Then, beginning with the president, each in turn kissed the book, and the court was in session.

The accused was offered an opportunity to introduce counsel, if he wished to employ any one in that capacity, but he declined the offer and sat down.

There were three charges, and to each charge one specification.

The charges were:

1st. Disobedience of orders.
2d. Drunkenness.
3d. Conduct unbecoming an officer and a gentleman.

It is unnecessary to state the specifications in the case. Each was an exact recital of the facts as given in the report of Captain Tempest, alleging that the accused had wilfully disobeyed his order, in not returning on board within the time directed. That when he did return he was intoxicated:—

And that the condition of his clothing and person was such, in addition to his intoxication, as to show conduct unbecoming an officer and a gentleman.

Called upon to hearken to the reading of the charges and specifications, the accused stood at attention, while they were read, and to each and all pleaded in a firm voice, 'Not Guilty.'

The court regarded the accused with interest. To most of them he was personally unknown. They saw a tall erect figure, with curly brown hair, well knit frame and a singularly intelligent countenance. A clear blue eye calmly looked upon the court, and none of the evasive glances of guilt could be discerned.

The prosecution then proceeded. Captain Tempest being called as a witness, and duly sworn by the president of the court, testified to giving the order putting the ship under sailing orders; to finding the accused missing at quarters in the morning; to his drunkenness on coming on board, and to his appearance generally. The captain gave his evidence with much emphasis, and regarded the accused sternly as he did so.

The lieutenant did not wish to cross-examine this witness, who, after approving his testimony, withdrew.

The executive officer testified to the same effect as the captain, except that he could not be certain as to the fact of intoxication.

The accused took a few notes, but did not cross-examine.

The court then adjourned, and as the flag was hauled down, a clipper schooner was seen entering the harbor, bringing the mails from the United States.

The one soft spot in Captain Tempest's soul, was love for his wife and daughter. The latter, a lovely girl of eighteen years was her father's idol. She was devoted to him, and could soothe and calm his fiercest moods; and there was nothing that he would not do at her bidding.

The captain sat in the cabin of his ship, on the evening of the day that he had given his evidence before the Court Martial, reading his letters from home. A shaded lamp shed a soft radiance about the place, and lighted up a pretty interior that was more like a boudoir on shore than the cabin of a ship. Loving hands had, with much care, added those soft touches which none but woman can give, and pretty articles of luxury and beauty were everywhere visible.

The captain opened a bulky letter in the delicate handwriting of his daughter. After detailing all the minute home news of friends and relatives, the letter went on as follows:

'After taking you to the wharf, dear Papa, in the carriage, the afternoon before you sailed, we stood on the Battery watching your boat until you reached the ship. Then Mamma and I looked at each other, and both burst into tears. We could not help it, Papa; we felt so very lonesome and desolate.

'The air was cold and piercing, and the horses seemed very restive. We did not notice it particularly, but after we had entered the carriage they started at a very rapid rate up Broadway, and we soon knew by the swaying of the vehicle that the horses were running away. We threw our arms about each other and clung convulsively, not knowing what our fate would be. Near Trinity Church our speed was abruptly checked, and then we stopped. We were helped from the carriage, and were so frightened that we took a hack standing near and hurried home, neither of us hurt, but frightened and excited very much.

'The carriage came home in a little while. One of the horses was hurt and lame, but is recovering now. What a narrow escape we had.

'But this is not all the story, and it seems wonderful sometimes, Papa, how things occur. Only think of it! we were saved from danger, and perhaps death, by one of the officers of your ship.

'The coachman said that after starting the horses took the bits in their teeth and began a mad run up Broadway. He could not control them. Suddenly a tall young man sprang at the head of the horse nearest him, caught the bridle, and held on with all his might. The horse soon fell, and we were horrified to hear that he had fallen upon our preserver, and that he was taken up insensible and carried into a neighboring drug store.

'Fancy our feelings! Mamma immediately sent for Uncle Tom, but he was away, and we could not see him until the next morning. He at once went in search of our deliverer, but found that he had left in haste, and that he was Lieutenant Singleton, of the *Champlain*.

'We were very sorry not to be able to express our gratitude to him, and fear very much that you sailed before he was able to get on board.

'Some gentlemen, friends of Uncle Tom, who saw the whole scene, say that Mr. Singleton acted with great bravery, and that he was severely injured.

'Uncle Tom went to Washington a day or two afterward and saw the Secretary of the Navy, and told him the whole story. Mr. Mason was much interested, and said that he would take such steps as were necessary, and that as Lieutenant Singleton had not reported to the Department, he had probably rejoined his ship before she sailed.'

When Captain Tempest had read so far in his daughter's letter, he stopped. His agitation was great. The officer whom he had relentlessly pursued in his strict interpretation of his duty, and of the maintenance of discipline, had actually saved his dear ones from injury, and perhaps death; had been severely hurt himself, and at the earliest moment had used every effort to rejoin his ship.

He saw it all now. He was a very proud man. To find himself in such a wrong position was a bitter experience to him. He recalled how his efforts had been used with the commander-in-chief to have the supposed culprit tried by court-martial, and had heaped indignity and official insult upon the preserver of his wife and daughter. He was utterly and absolutely in the wrong, and he knew it, and furthermore, everyone else must know it. Remorse and humiliation touched him to the heart.

While the captain was in this mental condition, the orderly entered the cabin, saluted, and presented a letter, saying, ' From the flag-ship, sir.'
Opening it he read the following:

NAVY DEPARTMENT, April 8th, 1844.

SIR:—The receipt of your letter to the Department, dated March 14th, in reference to Lieutenant Gustavus Singleton, is hereby acknowledged. The Department has been informed that the absence of Lieutenant Singleton on this occasion was caused by injuries received while performing an act of great personal bravery, whereby he probably saved the lives of two ladies, who proved to be your wife and daughter.

The Department highly appreciates the daring displayed by this officer upon the occasion mentioned, and desires that you will communicate to him its commendation for his conduct. Very respectfully,

J. R. MASON,
Secretary of the Navy.

CAPTAIN THOMAS TEMPEST, U. S. N.,
Commanding U. S. S. *Champlain* St. Thomas, West Indies.

The court-martial met the next morning pursuant to adjournment. The gun was again fired, the jack hoisted at the mizzen, and the accused presented himself before the court.

After the assembling of the members, the orderly informed the judge advocate that Captain Tempest desired a private interview with him. Retiring together, the captain laid before the officer of the court the communication from the Honorable Secretary of the Navy, and also informed him of the contents of his daughter's letter.

The judge advocate returned and addressed the court as follows:

' May it please the court, the prosecution will call no more witnesses, and will close its case here. It is entirely within the province of the court to call any witnesses at any time to make clear any desired point, but I do not think it will be necessary.

'Information has reached me that alters, very materially, the question and bearing of the charges and specifications, and it is necessary, for the just determination of the case, that evidence for the defense shall be introduced at once.'

At the suggestion of a member the court was cleared, and the judge advocate explained the new aspect of the case, and his course was approved.

The court was re-opened, and the first witness called was the surgeon, who testified most emphatically that the accused was not intoxicated at the time specified:— that when he fell upon the deck he had fainted from loss of blood and exhaustion :—and further, that from several years' acquaintance and association with him he knew Lieutenant Singleton to be an absolute teetotaler.

This evidence created some sensation in the court, and several members asked questions to make the evidence more exact and pertinent.

The judge advocate of a naval court-martial may act in a dual capacity. First, he is the prosecutor, and after the prosecution has closed, he may advise the accused as to his defense, if he has no counsel. That officer, therefore, retired with Mr. Singleton, and soon convinced him that his case could be left in the hands of the court.

Great was the astonishment among the spectators when the judge-advocate directed the orderly to call Captain Thomas Tempest as a witness for the defense.

The captain came gravely in, and took his seat as a witness before the court.

With a pale face and a quiet manner, Captain Tempest gave his evidence. He told of the news that he had received from home, that had led him to believe that his former conclusions in regard to the conduct of the accused had been wrong, and produced and offered in evidence the letter of the Secretary of the Navy, which was admitted and a copy appended to the record. The witness did not spare himself, and amid a breathless silence detailed the circumstances as described in the letter of his daughter. This was irregular evidence, but so great was the interest excited in the court, that it was decided to admit it, in order to make the case clear to the revising authority.

At the time of which I speak, the accused could not testify in his own behalf, a custom that is now changed. Lieutenant Singleton was unable to procure witnesses to testify for him in relation to the accident, but the letter of the Secretary of the Navy, an official paper, could be admitted, and was emphatic in its nature. A written defense, embodying all the facts of the case, was submitted to the court, and that body of officers unanimously declared the accused 'most honorably acquitted.'

The proceedings and finding of the court were promptly approved by the commander-in-chief, and promulgated in a general order to the squadron.

Two days afterward, on board the *Champlain* Captain Tempest ordered, 'All hands called to muster.'

The boatswain and his mates, with their shrill pipes, sounded 'Attention,' and then their hoarse summons: 'All hands to muster,' resounded through the ship.

The officers in undress uniform with swords assembled on the starboard side of the quarter deck. In the starboard waist the petty officers, neat and spotless in their attire, stood in two ranks. The marine guard, under arms, were on the port side of the quarter deck, while just forward of them was the remainder of the crew in four ranks.

All hands were reported ' up and aft.' The national standard floated from the mizzen peak. The decks were spotless in their purity. A row of glistening hammocks capped the rail on either side. Carefully spread awnings shaded the deck, while aloft the rigging and spars made accurate and sharply defined lines against the blue sky. The guns shone with their bright polish, and the brass work was refulgent in its brilliancy. It was a sight to charm a seaman's eye and heart, and was full of a romantic beauty that is now fast passing away.

In the midst of absolute stillness Captain Tempest came from his cabin and stepped upon the quarter deck. Officers and men uncovered and stood at attention.

After a short pause, the captain slowly and distinctly read the general order from the commander-in-chief, giving the decision of the court martial in the case of Lieutenant Singleton, and the flag-officer's approval thereof.

Then with a pale face and quivering lips, this violent but just officer spoke as follows :

' The order that I have just read has given to you all the official record of this case, in which, I am forced to confess, a gallant and meritorious officer was most unjustly brought to trial, and profoundly humiliated, mainly by my personal efforts.

' But there is another side to the matter, which concerns me alone. It is justice and a necessity, so the character of Lieutenant Singleton may be fully vindicated, that I should say before the officers and crew of this ship, who have witnessed his treatment at my hands, that my action was most unjust to him, and unmerited by him. In my earnest desire to maintain discipline, and to perform my duty as I understand it, I have wilfully injured the man who had ventured his life to preserve to me those whom I love dearer than life itself. I have deemed this public reparation due as well to him as to myself. Pipe down, sir.'

Captain Tempest turned away with a quivering lip to re-enter his cabin, and old Tommy Turner, the master-at-arms, sung out:

'Boys, we knows a man when we sees one. Three cheers for Captain Tempest.'"

The captain's story was received with great interest and applause, and, after a moment, he looked round for the next victim.

Somewhat to the right of the captain sat the fleet-paymaster,—Mr. Balance,—the only person on board with whom the captain could be said to be intimate. They had sailed with each other more than once before, and had a mutual respect, and even regard, which was rather unusual. So the captain, having been betrayed into giving a yarn, naturally wished to pass it on to his old shipmate.

The paymaster is a man of mature years, of quiet and unobtrusive manners, and a genial, pleasant nature. Exceeding liberal in his dealings with his shipmates (sometimes too much so for his own interests), he was a great favorite in the mess, but was seldom heard from as a "mess orator." *He* never was suspected of posting up on encyclopædias, or special works, and then cunningly leading the conversation to his point of departure. He never drank too much, but always enough, and was ready, every night, to smoke with the last man on the half-deck,—properly alleging that he had plenty of time for sleep.

The old fellow had a habit, derived from the custom obtaining during his early service, of sitting down at the wardroom table at seven bells in the forenoon with hard bread and cheese, and a black bottle supposed to contain "sherry" placed before him. His boy hovered about with the sugar-bowl and plated water-pitcher. First the paymaster would take a little nibble of bread and cheese, blandly addressing, meanwhile, any who might be near upon the news of the day,—purely local news, of course,—"galley news," indeed, when at sea. Then the paymaster would begin to mix a drink of amber liquid from the black bottle with sugar, water, and nutmeg, and then to stir it with his own particular spoon, —an apostle spoon, from his old place in Virginia (for the paymaster was really from one of the "first families," although not of the kind who are always letting you know about it).

Sometimes he would be heard to wish for mint and ice, all the time stirring his mixture, and smiling blandly on the society around him. Then he would taste it. Too much water, more "sherry." Then too much "sherry," very little more water. The same toddy all the time, for the dear old fellow prided himself upon never taking more than one. Before the end of the cruise his long apostle spoon, tinkling in his glass, was considered as good a mark of time as the deck time-

THE PAYMASTER'S STORY.

piece,—" It *must* be seven bells, for the paymaster is making his toddy."

When called upon for a yarn he modestly attempted to be exempted on account of the lateness of the hour. This was a ridiculous excuse to those who knew his habits, as every one then present of course did; for nowhere on this sphere is *one side* of a man better known than by those who sail with him. His futile attempt at excuse was promptly met by the captain, who had just then lighted his fourth cigar, and had nodded at the first lieutenant, who, in his turn, had nodded at the master-at-arms,—that ubiquitous functionary having just then appeared at the wardroom door again with his " Ten o'clock, gentlemen."

When the master-at-arms had retired,—evidently under protest, and with a strong conviction that the service was going to the devil,—Mr. Balance said,—

" Well, I *do* remember one Christmas eve which was a serious time for me, and during which, indeed, I came very near losing the number of my mess. I dare say I have told the story to you before, but as there are some here who certainly have not heard it, I will tell it again.

The incident occurred in China,—the very station we have so lately left. I was then attached to the ' Kiskiminetas,' a fine, comfortable, roomy, old-fashioned sloop-of-war. In those days members of my corps were still called pursers. It was before Japan was opened by Commodore Perry, and our vessels spent most of the time in the Canton waters,—between Macao, Whampoa, and the new English town of Hong-Kong,—with an occasional trip to Shanghai, Amoy or Manilla, when the monsoon served. These visits were looked upon as quite a cruise, for we had no steamer on the station then. But the ships composing the squadron were always in splendid order, and, if the duty was easy-going, and even a little sleepy, we could do sailor-work when the occasion required. We used to back and fill all the way through the mass of shipping in Whampoa Reach, and never graze another ship. We used to furl all sail together, from studding-sails, and make a flying moor at the same time; and all in a way that would surprise the present generation.

The officers then wore big topped caps, with a wide gold band, and no device, and swallow-tailed coats, with buttons on the hips and cuffs. Jack wore sennit hats or tarpaulins always. Caps were then only surreptitiously introduced by progressive captains and first lieutenants."

"And a bad thing, too," interjected Captain Tangent; "no sailor-men since that time."

"The Taë-ping rebellion," continued the paymaster, "was then in its very inception, and the populace of Canton, where our principal interests then were, was very unruly and dangerous, rendering it almost impossible to leave Whampoa, even for a day or two, without a man-of war there ready for emergencies. The Chinese would not allow any white man to enter the walls of any of the towns, and the walks of foreigners were confined to a few lanes of shops in the immediate vicinity of the foreign factories at Canton. Indeed, many Americans and English were seriously injured, and some even killed for transgressing these bounds.

The river was full of skulking robbers and pirates, and mysterious disappearances were not unfrequent, especially among the foreigners who inhabited the floating houses and hulks moored at Whampoa, which habitations belonged to the brokers, ship-chandlers, sail-makers and others, who depended upon the large business brought by the immense number of vessels which then came to that one port for tea cargoes. The 'Tea Fleet' it was called,—the finest vessels of the whole being our own unrivaled clippers,—such as the *Sea Witch*, the *Sea Serpent*, the *Challenge*, the *N. B. Palmer*, the *Sam Russell*, and many others. No such ships had ever been seen before in any part of the world, and no passages like theirs had ever been made. The *Stornaway* and many other Scotch clippers were built to rival them, but when it came to a tea-race to London, the Yankee clipper generally took the annual reward.

The boat-work of vessels on that station was seldom done by the ship's boats,—on account of the deleterious influences of climate and *samshu*,—and all men-of-war had a 'fast-boat,'—a masted, half-decked, native craft, generally of some size, and carrying a head-man and a crew of eight or ten sturdy fellows. This boat was usually owned by the head-man, and lay moored at the stern buoy ready for any service, night or day. The head-man of our boat bore the very common name of Assam,—a muscular, broad-faced, bronzed, good-natured fellow, most obliging and useful, and an excellent boatman. His little wife, Ati, was worth more than two of him, however. She generally took charge of the boat, —her face always wreathed in smiles, her hair neatly dressed, and her scanty but decent dress starched and clean. She cooked the men's rice, scrubbed every plank in the boat every day, and attended to her baby beside,—a little chap about a year old, who was generally slung at her back, and whose shaven head wabbled about in the blazing sun as his mother stood at the great sculling-oar, scarcely able to grasp the loom with her little brown hands, gay with brass rings.

On account of the bad characters generally to be found upon the river at night, it was usual, in going to Canton from Whampoa, either for business or pleasure, to take a tide which was favorable during daylight. Otherwise, on account of the sun, it would have been much more pleasant to select the hours of darkness.

Early on the morning of the day before Christmas, 18—, I started for Canton with the tide in our fast-boat, —my object being to obtain ' chop dollars' in exchange for a draft on Barings' for two thousand pounds,— partly for ship's expenses, and partly to enable me to pay the men their monthly money and stopped rations, and, by advancing the money, to enable them to keep the holiday properly. I was accompanied by our assistant surgeon and one of the midshipmen,—these young gentlemen wishing to go shopping in Canton and buy some *curios* for their friends and sweethearts.

A sergeant and four marines were ordered to accompany me,—with muskets, bayonets, and forty rounds,—a usual precaution when carrying money in that part of the world, as it was impossible to make a secret of the big bags of silver carried down to the boat on coolies' shoulders. As was usual, also, some pieces of small-stuff, fitted with wooden buoys, were taken along, to be made fast to the bags, as a precaution in case of a capsize or other accident.

We reached Canton about ten o'clock in the forenoon,

without other incident than the seeing, and smelling, of four ghastly heads stuck upon poles just at the water's edge, where a narrow but deep creek emptied into the river. 'Four piecee dead man,' Assam said they were, which was evident to more than one sense. They were the heads of 'ladrones,' or river-pirates, who had lately robbed a boat at that place. Not that it at all followed that they were precisely the people who had committed the offense, but, as the Chinese police had been commanded to make an example, they had decapitated four fellows who *might* have committed the act, and here were their heads.

In those days the influx of two or three strangers at 'tiffin' made no great demand upon the proverbial hospitality of the foreign 'factories' at Canton, but was rather welcomed as a pleasant break in the monotony of the lives led by the merchants, tea-tasters, and clerks. As soon, therefore, as I had transacted my business belowstairs, we ascended to the first floor of the commodious establishment of Russell & Company, and, after an interchange of news and gossip, were soon seated at a sumptuous and welcome luncheon.

While thus pleasantly engaged I received a 'chit' from down below, informing me that the 'shroff' had some difficulty in raising the amount of coin I needed at such short notice, but would hurry the business as much as possible. Uneasy, and anxious to be off, I left the table as soon as I could, and sauntered down toward the boat. There were the marines, just where I had left them, all right, perfectly sober, and having a comfortable smoke, while they chaffed the group of Chinamen and Parsees who were gazing on them from the 'bund.' At last, about four o'clock, the money came down, borne upon the shoulders of several trotting coolies, marshaled by the solemn old 'shroff,' with his slender pig-tail, long finger-nails, and immense spectacles looped behind his ears.

The tide was now more than three-quarters done, and less than two hours of daylight remained. Perhaps it would have been wiser to remain at the factories all night, especially as intelligence of any movement is conveyed by the swarming river population with marvelous speed, but I was very anxious to get down to the ship, knowing how the money was looked for by the men, and also desirous of having my business over, and being thus enabled to attend a grand Christmas 'tiffin' on board the *Commodore*, and dine in our own pleasant mess in the evening. I was younger then, and was willing to take more risks, and so I resolved to start.

When all was ready, and the bags properly buoyed and stowed under the cockpit, I was delayed by the vexatious disappearance of my companions, who had strolled out again to the lanes of shops, promising to be back 'in ten minutes.' We all know what a youngster's 'ten minutes' are. Messengers were sent for them, but they did not appear until near five, being then very profuse in apologies for delaying me. At last we shoved off, almost at the last of the ebb. It was dead calm, and the crowd of boats and junks of all sorts, which literally covered the stream for a long distance down, rendered our progress so slow that it was a good half-hour before the men could settle down for a steady pull.

The sun soon went down, and the night came on with the suddenness peculiar to the latitude. It became very dark and overcast, and Assam, in answer to my inquiry, said he thought the tide was done, and that we would meet the flood before we reached the Barrier Forts. I saw from his manner that the man was uneasy. Every now and then, at a muttered word from him, the crew would cease pulling and listen intently, when a belated fast-boat or sampan would be heard approaching in the darkness, and a mutual hail would pass, our men then giving way again, evidently very much relieved.

Little Ati all this time stood at the steering-oar, her baby sound asleep at her feet in a bundle of cloths. Ati did all the hailing, and was virtually captain of the craft, for honest old Assam trusted more to her eyes and ears than his own, and tugged away manfully at the stroke-oar. Hugging the right bank as our guide, we had nearly reached the creek where we had seen the dead men's heads that morning, when Assam, after a word from Ati, held up his hand for a moment's silence. Then he suddenly hissed out to his crew to give way strong, and at that moment the rest of us heard the plash of many oars coming down the creek and the creaking noise of the bamboo grummets in which the oars were pulled.

As our boat, with freshened way, darted across the mouth of the creek, we could dimly perceive a long, snaky, ' pull-away boat,' such as the ladrones used. These boats are very fast, and often carry forty or fifty desperate, opium-soaked ruffians, armed to the teeth. Revolvers were not then used in the navy, but we all had pistols of the old type, which were noted for never hitting anything, with their big round balls, at more than five paces. We got them out, however, and the old sergeant, was as cool as his bayonet, stood up with his four men and covered the advancing boat, ready to fire at the word. It was a comfort to see the old fellow take it as a part of the day's work and of the duty he had been sent upon. Thinking it possible it might be a mandarin-boat, or patrol (although they did not bear the best reputation, and a boat with Fanquis and dollars was a great temptation), still, to be sure, I said to Ati, who was steering a straight course and perfectly cool,—

'Hail them, Ati.'

This she shrilly did, and was answered by a volley of Chinese oaths and anathemas, and by an ominous clash of knives and swords.

'Him say stop! S'pose hab throat cut,' said Ati.

'Fire, sir?' said the sergeant, calmly sighting just over our heads as we stood in the cockpit.

'Fire, sergeant!'—and we could hear the balls strike the planking of the strange boat, now very near us, and a yell, as of some one badly hit, while our fire evidently caused some confusion and a temporary increase of distance between us. In a moment, however, they came on again, with yells and curses, while the many oars tossed the water into foam, and our own men, with set teeth and heavy breath, and bare heels fairly straining the stretchers, pulled for their lives.

'Fire again, sergeant! Pull, Assam! Hold your pistol-fire, boys! If we allow them to get alongside they'll cut all our throats.'

Apparently they were only four or five boats' lengths off, our men pulling desperately, but losing all the time, when I remembered the money. Determined that they should not get that at any rate, I raised the hatch, and, with the help of my companions, quietly eased the heavy bags overboard. The youngsters at the same time dropped the treasured bronzes and other *curios* which they had bought that day. At the very moment we did so I became aware that our foes were dropping astern, leaving us, in fact, about as rapidly as they had been approaching. Looking round, I beheld another boat, pulling at least forty oars, coming obliquely across the river, her outline shown by the bright light of several lanterns, which disclosed, beside the rowers, a fellow high up in the stern, who began to pound away on a gong as if his life depended upon it.

'He mandarin-boat,' said Assam, when the stranger hailed us; 'wanchee stop,—occasion talkee.'

Darting by us up-stream at a tremendous rate, we saw him soon overhaul the ladrone, the crew of which ran her ashore and took to the swamp, but not before about a dozen of them had been captured, two of them so badly wounded by our fire that they could not attempt to escape. With the pirate-boat in tow, the mandarin-boat now pulled down to the spot where we had run the fast-boat's nose upon the mud, forced down a bamboo, and made the painter fast. After explaining the whole affair, through Assam and Ati, who fairly cowered before the officer, he said that he had just patrolled from the neighborhood of Whampoa, and that no ladrones were likely to be below that night.

While thus conversing with him we heard the unmistakable regular beat of a double-banked man-of-war's boat coming up the stream, and almost immediately, to my great joy, the hail of a familiar voice. In a moment there shot within the circle of light our first cutter, with the senior passed midshipman (who, poor fellow, was killed at New Orleans afterwards) standing in the stern-sheets; six marines, with their polished musket-barrels, surrounded him, while sixteen bronzed sailors, with pistol and cutlass belted on, were just tossing their oars. Mr. Vang soon explained that the captain, rendered anxious by our non-appearance before dark, had dispatched the armed boat to meet us, and that they had come up rapidly with the young flood. The Chinese officer, rather a young man, and a good type of the military mandarin, with his blue button, hearty bronzed face, and alert, pleasant manner, now prepared to depart for Canton with his prisoners and the ladrone-boat in tow. The wounded men had been attended to by the assistant surgeon,—rather against the wishes of the officer, who seemed to think it very unnecessary trouble; and he soon shoved off, and disappeared around a bend in the river.

By this time it was almost ten o'clock. All river traffic had entirely ceased for the night, and the stream, which was such a thoroughfare by day, was now as still and silent as the grave. I mentioned to Vang that about ten thousand dollars, in bags, were now reposing at the bottom of the river. Lighting lanterns, we put the marines on post on the embankment abreast of us, for fear of another visit of ladrones, at once proceeded to search for the small buoys, and after a long time, discovered and raised all the bags but one. Of this the buoy-rope had either slipped, or the buoy itself was run under by the tide, which was now strong flood. Making fast again to the bank,—as near as possible to the place where we supposed the bag to be,—we stretched out under the awnings to wait for daylight and slack water. There was bread and a beaker of water in the cutter, and we passed a long, dreary night in nibbling hard-tack and dozing.

I must say that I did not sleep much—not particularly on account of the missing sum for which I was responsible as because I blamed myself for starting down the river with treasure at so late an hour, and thus putting the lives of myself and so many others in such fearful jeopardy. Finally, however, thankfulness for our escape from such a death as these pirates would have inflicted became uppermost in my mind, and seemed to render the money responsibility very light. It had, indeed, been a narrow shave for us.

At last the day broke, with a sickening, malarious fog and disagreeable odor arising from the paddy-fields, which admonished us to be off as soon as possible. By the very first tanka-boat which came stealing along through the mist we sent a note down to the captain, with promise of a dollar to the boat people if it was delivered soon, and then we went to work to try to recover the missing bag. The tide being by this time ebb again, the cutter and fast-boat swept up river with a loaded line to endeavor to entangle the buoy which was supposed to be ridden under by the tide; but, after a long trial, we reluctantly came to the conclusion that there had been a 'slippery hitch,' and that there was no buoy there.

While consulting as to further operations, Assam came to us and said that his wife would like to make an effort to recover the bag by diving. Like most Tanka women, Ati swam like a fish, and we very gladly availed ourselves of her proffered services. Anchoring the fast-boat just above where the bag was supposed to be lying, the little woman carefully unslung and packed away her long-suffering and patient baby. She then made a bowline in one of the halliards, and gave her husband a coil of the same to hold, stripped to her broad trousers, and dove straight down. The depth was only about two fathoms, but the water very muddy, as it always is there. In a short time she reappeared, the beads of water rolling off her tawny, firm, velvety skin, as she climbed into the boat, where she appeared entirely unconscious that the 'pijammas' were showing the full outline of her shapely lower limbs. In fact, she was now thoroughly excited, and, with her nervous, agile movements and glittering eye, put one in mind of an otter emerging from his favorite element.

Quickly causing them to drop the boat about a length (the men always obeyed her rather more quickly than Assam), she dove in again like a beaver, remaining this time about a minute. Thrice she repeated this operation, shifting the position of the boat a very little each time, until, finally, Assam, who was 'twiddling' at the slack of the line, suddenly sang out 'Can secure!'

Sure enough! When Ati appeared above the surface again, and had recovered her breath, she grinned so as to show all her white teeth, and laughed out, 'Haul away! Can secure!' The bowline was indeed round the bag, and the dollars were soon lying in the bottom of the boat,—covered with river ooze to be sure, but safe enough.

Long before this time the river was alive with cargo-boats and sampans, and a vigorous cross-examination was made of our Chinamen by each passing craft, re-

THE PAYMASTER'S STORY. 65

sponded to by our fellows at the top of their voices, after the manner of Chinese watermen. No doubt some of the passers were fellows of the marauders who had attacked us during the previous night, and they knew perfectly well that in those two boats we had what was to them great treasure, but daylight, and our numbers and firearms, removed any apprehension of attack from any source.

Having satisfied myself that the bags were all right, we gave away down the river, and found ourselves safe on board in a couple of hours. My first business, of course, was to lock up the wet bags, and then to report in writing the details of yesterday's proceedings, which occupied considerable time, so that I did not go to the 'tiffin' after all. A bath and a good nap put me in readiness for our own Christmas dinner, however, which I enjoyed the more from not having been at the 'tiffin.'

Before dinner I sent for Ati to come on board. She had never been upon our deck, some sense of propriety restraining her, and when she came it was difficult to get her to go below, although she knew us all very well. When she came down and was seated, I told her that this was 'Big Joss day! Alla same China New-Year!' and then I made her supremely happy with as many of the 'chop' dollars as she could scoop up and carry in her two hands. Wages in China were excessively low, and what I gave her was a small fortune to her, and went very far towards building a larger and better boat, in which they would get the service of a frigate.

Not long after this event, in fact, just at New-Year, our captain received, through the consul, a formal message from the Tautaë, or governor of Canton, to say that the pirates who had been taken at the time of their attack upon us were to be executed upon the spot where the offense had been committed, and the governor requested that we should send some witnesses on our part to the bona fides of the Chinese authorities in punishing pirates. Accordingly, two cutters with their crews, and four or five officers with side-arms, were at the spot I knew so well at the time appointed in the consul's note.

We had not long landed on the levée, or embankment, when a mandarin-boat, with streamers flying and gongs beating, as was their custom then, came dashing down the stream, her many oars making her look like a centipede. The officer in charge stood upon the poop, and shook his own hands, and exchanged ceremonial 'chin-chins' and formal bows with our party. Then the prisoners were brought out, and marched on shore with their hands tied behind their back. They looked like common river people, only very dirty and emaciated, from the days spent in a Chinese prison, where they had been crowded, starved, and eaten by vermin. They were, to all outward appearance, entirely unconcerned, however, and did not raise their eyes nor utter a word.

Without any reading of warrant, or more ado of any kind, they were caused to kneel in a row at the side of the pathway along the top of the embankment. A man then passed along, firmly pressing their heads toward the ground, and throwing the plait, or 'pig-tail,' of each one forward, so as to reach the ground in front. Each criminal's hands rested on his knees. At a sign from the mandarin the executioner—a fat, brawny, good-natured-looking old fellow, in no way differing in dress or appearance from those about him, except that he was stouter, and had a short, ragged cue—stepped to the left of the first man, and, with an instrument something between a broadsword and a cleaver,—exceedingly heavy and sharp,—struck off his head at a blow.

Not a movement was made by the next man, though he must have seen, or at least heard, the cleaver chopping off his fellow's head. In a few seconds his own followed, and rolled down the bank. So expert was the executioner that eleven were thus put to death in less time than I have taken to tell about it, and almost all had their heads cleanly cut off. These were all gathered, and planted along the dyke on bamboos. What became of the bodies I don't know. They were all lying there, with the blow-flies already upon them, when we left the spot."

"Speaking of the impassable conduct of Chinamen in such circumstances," said the fleet-surgeon, when the paymaster had finished his story, "reminds me of the four Chinamen who were executed by the English authorities at Green Point, Hong-Kong, just before we sailed. As I was taking an early morning walk in that direction, I was attracted by the small cortege, and approached the place. They were to be hung on four separate gallows. Few Chinamen were present, and those of the very lowest class. About a dozen sepoy or Cingalese policemen formed the escort, and one of them acted as executioner. There appeared to be only two white men there,—a sort of sheriff and his deputy,—who had general charge.

When all was ready, and the signal given, three of the culprits were dropped at once, and seemed to expire without a struggle. But the pin holding the platform under the fourth one was jammed,—owing to rust and neglect,—and did not yield until after some minutes' pounding with a stone from the shingle beach. The curious part of the whole affair was that the fourth Chinaman, standing there with his eyes unbandaged and the halter round his neck, merely patted his foot and said several times, and in rather a petulant tone, ' Fi-tee !' Hurry !

The whole proceeding was beastly, and put one in mind of the slaughter of animals, and was not really so efficient, or so humane, as the decapitation which the paymaster has just described."

"Mr. Balance, by the way, had even a narrower squeak than our purser had, when I was out there in the 'M——,' in 1850," said the captain. "He was coming from Hong-Kong with a good deal of money, in dollars, to our ship, at Cum-singmoon. Two ladrone-boats chased him through the passages in broad daylight. They came out from the clefts of the rocky, perpendicular cliffs, and he was only saved by suddenly coming, at an abrupt turn of the passage, upon a large bark at anchor and waiting the tide. The skipper of the bark, a bright fellow, promptly took in the situation, and trained his six-pounder upon the rascals, when they quickly vanished behind the rocks again. Our purser then wisely stuck to the bark, which towed him up within sight of our ship before casting him off."

Intently listening to the paymaster's old-world story was a lieutenant seated to the right of the admiral, Burton by name, sometimes called "Spanish Burton," on account of his dark eyes, complexion, and hair. His eyes had been fixed upon a raisin in a heel-tap of champagne, rising with its load of gas, discharging it, and descending again for a fresh supply; and one would have supposed he was thinking of nothing else, when he suddenly pushed the glass away, and addressing the last speaker, said, " I would like to relate a story."

" Go on, Mr. Burton, by all means," said the caterer.

" Well, it is a story of love and faith,—a story of one we called ' Queen Annie:'—

The United States ship *Atchafalaya*, in the summer of 1864, was cruising off the Atlantic coast of the United States with the object of picking up any thing that might offer in the way of a prize but with particular orders to look out for the rebel cruiser *Tallahassee*, supposed to be in those waters.

The wardroom dinner was just over and the officers were cracking nuts and jokes, the latter venerable enough to have earned the sobriquet of ' chestnut ' had that phrase been then invented. The paymaster had told the forgetful-man's story for the seventeenth time, one of the acting masters had related his experience on a whaler with an accuracy born of long practice and a careful study of Herman Mellville, and the Doctor was clearing his voice to begin an account of an amputation of the hip joint so familiar to his mess-mates that most of them could have performed it, if not as skillfully, at least with as good results as the Doctor himself since, by his own admission, the patient died.

Joe Graydon the handsome navigator of the ship was startled from a gentle doze into which these barnacle backed narratives had lulled him, by a hail from the main top which came floating down the open skylight.

'There's something looks like a boat on the weather bow, sir.'

In less time than it takes to tell it Joe was in the top with his binocular at his eye.

'What do you make of her Mr. Graydon ?' hailed the captain from the bridge.

'She is a boat right enough, sir,' was the answer, 'and—and—yes with people in her' then, after a pause, 'By Jove I almost think I can make out a woman's dress.'

'Keep the ship off and run down to her, Mr. Smith,' said the Captain quietly to the officer of the deck and a few minutes later Joe who had kept his eyes glued to his binocular, hailed

'By Jove, sir, it is a woman, sure as you're born, sir, it's a woman.'

Orders were given to clear away the second cutter and Joe's offer to go in charge of her was accepted.

'Give way men, give way for your lives' was Graydon's order as they shoved off, and give way they did though, as they approached them, the wrecked crew did not seem to be suffering any great hardship. The boat was found to contain a bluff weather-beaten old captain, four hale and hearty-looking seamen and last but not least, so far as my story is concerned for without her it would not have been told was the girl. I wish I could describe her as she sat there in the stern sheets looking as calm and collected as if she were out for a summer's afternoon sail. It warms the cockles of my old heart now as I see her come over the gangway of the *Atchafalaya*. She was not one of those beauties with black eyes, raven locks and, *entre nous*, a deuce of a temper, about which poets rave, but her figure was petite, with hands so small that when I gave them a fatherly squeeze, and I was old enough to feel that I had a perfect right to do so, they were lost in my great red flipper, her feet—such feet—

> 'That 'neath her petticoats
> Like little mice crept in and out.'

Her features, as I have been told by several amiable ladies, were not regular, her cheeks were too red, her mouth too large, her ears too small, her teeth, well they must have been too white, and one feline female spoke of her red hair but it was such red as Titian loved to paint. I am not prepared to dispute the good ladies referred to with regard to the individual features but combined they certainly formed the loveliest face it had ever been my good fortune to look upon. She was the daughter of Geoffrey La Cour, one of New York's merchant princes, a widower who idolized his two children. The boy had utilized some nautical knowledge gained on his father's yacht in obtaining an appointment as master's mate in the Navy. Mr. La Cour having some business in San Domingo and knowing little of that island unwisely took his daughter Annie with him but, finding it no place for her, sent her home in a small brig loaded with logwood and mahogany, the only vessel then bound for the States. The brig caught fire four days before we picked up the boat. The crew took to the boats; one in charge of the mate, was lost sight of the first night, but was afterwards picked up by a homeward bound steamer; the other was out four days but, as the weather was good and she was well provided with water and provisions the castaways suffered no great hardship.

The rescue proved a blessing to us, as we were shorthanded, and the four sailors, out of a job, gladly signed the ship's articles, while the captain volunteered to stand the watch of a sick officer, which he did so efficiently that when he reached port he was recommended for and received the appointment of acting master. As for little Annie, she took up her quarters in the captain's spare state-room and her position as queen of the ship. Indeed, in less than a week she was known fore and aft as 'Queen Annie,' and I verily believe that had her will run counter to that of the Secretary of the Navy, the captain would not have hesitated to obey it, and as for the men, though the *Atchafalaya* was a well-disciplined ship, she had but to say the word and a mutiny would have followed. She took her dainty little meals with the utmost impartiality in the cabin or in the ward room, and the two stewards vied with each other in devising delicate sea-messes which gladdened the hearts of the officers.

Fortunately the captain's wife, who was in Europe, had left a couple of trunks in the cabin to save storage, so that her majesty, with some assistance from her deft needle, was well provided with royal robes. Joe Graydon, as the youngest and handsomest man in the ship, naturally dropped into the position of prime minister, and never was a minister more devoted to his royal mistress. No sooner did she poke her pretty little nose out of the cabin door than he was by her side; he walked with her, talked with her, waited on her, brought her shawls when she was cold and fanned her when warm, and all this he did not only cheerfully but joyfully, for he had learned

THE LIEUTENANT'S STORY.

to love 'Queen Annie' with the whole of his big, noble heart. An obstacle, however, came into Joe's mind which a less scrupulous man would have pushed aside or considered an advantage. Annie was, or would be, rich, while Joe had not a cent except his lieutenant's pay. A kind old uncle had supported him and his sister Nettie until, on his graduation from the academy, he was able to do so himself, and having come into possession of several thousand dollars prize money, he deemed it his duty, Quixotically, Nettie thought, to return this money to his uncle, who, while he did not ask it, did not refuse it. Joe had always made a confidant of me, and after imparting the above particulars one night in the midwatch, he said:

'What right have I to drag such a woman into poverty, and what right have I, coxcomb that I am, to believe that this peerless woman cares for me except as an instrument to while away the tedium of an involuntary sea voyage.'

'There is a quotation trite but true,' said I:

> 'He either fears his fate too much,
> Or his deserts are small,
> Who fears to put it to the touch
> And win or lose it all.'

'Aye, my dear old friend,' said Joe, 'and I would put it to the touch, but for another quotation as trite and true as yours:

> 'I could not love her half so much,
> Loved I not honor more.'

I cannot imagine anything meaner than to ask this dear girl to join her fate to one who has so little to offer in return, simply because I have been able to take her from a boat without any danger to myself and render her some little attention for which she is unduly grateful.'

I could make no answer to this, and poor Joe continued to singe his wings in the light of 'Queen Annie's' smiles.

The weather up to this time had been faultless, but now the sky betokened a storm, and before night it came piping out of the northeast. The sails were furled, fires spread, topmast housed, yards lowered on the caps and every preparation made for a gale. The sky was black as ink, the mountain waves capped with snowy foam which drifted before the wind, forming the grandest sight given to those 'who go down to the sea in ships,' but one which most seamen would willingly forego. As I was hurrying aft in the pursuit of my duty I noticed Annie standing under the break of the poop; her arm was thrown around a stanchion and the wind was playing havoc with her lovely tresses, but the roses on her cheeks were deepened rather than diminished, and the wonted smile parted her lips.

'You do not seem alarmed, Miss Annie,' said I.

'No,' was her smiling reply, 'why should I be? The ship is stanch, the officers and crew know their duty and will protect their queen and,' dropping her playful tone, 'the same Providence watches over us on water as on land.'

For three days and nights the gale blew with terrible force. Seldom have I seen a fiercer one, but through it all the brave girl was calm and smiling, and many a wet and weary sailor remembers to this day how he was cheered and encouraged by her words and actions.

At last the storm was over and the bright sun came out again. Scarcely had the ship been put in order when the hail, always exciting at sea, of 'Sail ho!' was heard from aloft.

'Where away?' from the officer of the deck.

'Right ahead, sir; looks like a man-o'-war.'

'Take a look at her, Mr. Graydon,' said the captain, who was on the bridge. And after Joe had gone aloft with his glass: 'What do you make of her, sir?'

'She is certainly a man-'o-war, sir; about the size, I should think of the *Tallahassee*, and is steaming slowly across our bows as if waiting for us.'

'So,' remarked the skipper, 'he wants a fight, does he? Well, he shall have it. Beat to quarters and clear the ship for action.'

Now all was excitement without the slightest confusion. The drum beat to quarters and each man went to his station as quietly as if he was going there for drill, though all of them expected to be in the midst of death and carnage in a few minutes. Then the decks were strewn with sand to absorb the blood which was to flow, and all was ready for the conflict. Joe Graydon had just left the poop where he had been to receive some final instruction when, coming out of the cabin door, he met 'Queen Annie.' There was no smile on her lips now, her cheeks were pale as death and she trembled like an aspen. 'Oh, Mr. Graydon,' she exclaimed with tears in her voice which overflowed and dropped from her eyes; 'Oh, Mr. Graydon, are we going to have a battle?'

'I fear so,' said Joe; 'and I am very sorry for your sake. You had better go into the hold, it is not very comfortable, but below the water line and comparatively safe. I will ask the captain to let me take you there.'

'Safe!' exclaimed she, 'do you think I am a coward to run away from danger to which you—to which,' with a blush, 'my friends are exposed? I do not fear for myself, but for those I love.'

We continued to steam down towards the other vessel, which still kept broadside to us until we made out her ensign, which, to the disgust of every one except Annie, proved to be the stars and stripes; but it was worth the disappointment to see the light come back to our darling's eyes and hear her merry laugh ring through the ship once more. The vessel we took for the *Tallahassee* was one of the ninety-day gunboats, as they were called, which had been sent out to find us and deliver orders for us to proceed to Norfolk, there to refit, preparatory to the contemplated expedition against Fort Fisher. Under ordinary circumstances this news would have been hailed with delight, but, since it involved parting from our 'Queen,' I verily believe every soul in the ship, from the captain to the cook, would have preferred remaining at sea; but there was no help for it, so we steered for the capes of the Chesapeake, and in three or four days, after barely stopping, without letting go our anchor, at Hampton Roads, to communicate with the admiral, we reached Norfolk Navy Yard. Here Annie telegraphed to know whether her father had returned from San Domingo. He had; and had also learned from the mate of the burning of the brig and the separation of the boats, but no more; therefore his joy knew no bounds when he learned of his daughter's safety, and not many hours elapsed before he arrived in

Norfolk. He proved a dignified old gentleman full of gratitude, and brimming over with the milk of human kindness. I think he would have liked to have devoted half his fortune to the crew; and the canvas-backs, terrapins, Lynn Haven oysters, champagne and other luxuries that he lavished upon the officers unfitted them for the wardroom mess for months afterwards. His son, Charley, who was attached to one of the ships at Hampton Roads, got a couple of days' leave to visit his father and sister. We made him a wardroom officer with an occasional meal in the cabin, for nothing was too good for 'Queen Annie's' brother, or 'Prince Charley,' as we called him. But kind and hospitable as Mr. La Cour was, we would have been willing to forego it all if he could have spared us our darling, but this, of course, was impossible, and, all too soon, the afternoon came when she was to leave us. All hands were called and our 'Queen' stood upon the horse-block to bid us farewell.

'Messmates and shipmates,' she said, 'I am about to bid you farewell. I do not know how to thank you for all that you have done for me. I—' and the tears fell thick and fast; in vain she tried to recover herself until she gave up the effort, and her whole frame shook and trembled with her sobs. There was not a dry eye in the ship, and many a weather-beaten old seaman wept like a child. At length she became somewhat calmer, and, after shaking hands with every man in the ship, returned on Joe Graydon's arm to the cabin. She went on board the boat in the gig with her father, the dear old captain himself steering the boat, while the rest of us followed in the first cutter.

Why dwell upon that sad parting? Enough that she sailed away and Joe Graydon, whose love of honor was greater than love itself, uttered no word. Joe was not one 'to wear his heart upon his sleeve,' and no one except myself, I being, as I have said, his confidant, knew the sacrifice he had made. Perhaps he was less gay and playful and less fond of amusements than of old, but the executive officer was sent to the hospital with a sprained ankle about this time, and as Joe had to take his place in fitting out the ship, his duties became so important that he had little time for amusement, and those duties were performed as conscientiously and thoroughly as ever.

At length our repairs were completed. The executive officer, though still a little lame, managed to get discharged from the hospital and we joined the fleet in Hampton Roads, whence we soon sailed for Fort Fisher.

The fierce bombardment of the 24th-25tn of December, successful as a bombardment but useless in its result, has nothing to do with my story, and I have no intention of describing it. It is sufficient to say that after it was over we withdrew temporarily to Port Royal, where after repairing damages, we returned, when, on the 15th of January, 1865, a land attack was made by the sailors and marines on foot, which proved one of the bloodiest and most disastrous of the war. The detachment from the *Atchafalaya* was commanded by Joe Graydon. On reaching shore the men were formed, and marched across the beach, to face such a fire as few men have ever been called upon to encounter. Time after time they were hurled against the fort only to be forced back with terrible loss, while their sheltered foe was utterly unharmed. At last the order was given to retreat, but by that time it had ceased to be a battle and became a massacre ; what with death and demoralization there were few left to retreat, and every man shifted for himself. As Joe retraced his steps through that hell of fire, he noticed that some of his own men had thrown up a small breastworks of sand to form a partial protection against the fire of the enemy. When within about a hundred yards of this shelter a young officer, hardly more than a boy, passing within a few yards of him, threw up his hands and fell forward upon the sand. Though every moment's delay was fraught with terrible danger, Joe unhesitatingly knelt beside the wounded man and recognized the features of Charley La Cour. 'Leave me, Mr. Graydon and save yourself,' said the brave boy. But Joe Graydon was not the person to desert any man under such circumstances, and certainly not ' Queen Annie's ' brother, so he hoisted him upon his back while Charley set his teeth with pain but uttered no cry. He struggled through the sand with bullets screaming and whistling all around, but not one harmed them, though two pierced the visor of Joe's cap and several went through Charley's coat. At last they reached the breastwork and were in comparative safety, where, the men all being 'Atchafalayas,' Charley was as welcome as Graydon himself. Joe was delighted to find that Charley's wound was no more serious than a ball through the fleshy part of the leg, which he bound up as best he could with his handkerchief until he was able to reach the beach and convey his patient on board the *Atchafalaya*, where he surrendered his own room, and the good old doctor could hardly have been more attentive had the case involved his pet amputation of the hip joint. As our ship had been considerably damaged during the bombardment, it was decided to send her to Norfolk with such of the less severely wounded as had not gone to the hospital immediately after the engagement. Charley was one of them, and, of course, he continued to occupy Joe's room while its owner deemed it a privilege to swing in a cot for his accommodation. As soon as she heard of our arrival Annie came down to meet her brother, but he did not require her services, and the hospital was so crowded that the doctors discouraged very frequent visits. So, as Yankees were not looked on with much favor there, her principal amusements were long walks with Joe. The scenery around Norfolk and Portsmouth is not very romantic, but with ' Queen Annie ' for a companion Joe found the dusty roads, corn fields and truck patches more attractive than the wildest glades in the Adirondacks. But all this could not last. Charley was soon able to hobble on board the Old Dominion steamer and sail away with ' Queen Annie ' for their home in New York.

It was found that the *Atchafalaya* needed so many repairs that, as the war was virtually over, it was deemed best to put her out of commission. So the old ship went into rotten-row and many dear friends parted— some of them forever. Joe went to the little nest he had built for himself and Nettie on Long Island. He loved his sister dearly, and though, had he not been blinded by his affection for her, he would hardly have gone to her for sympathy, he needed it so much that he could not help thinking that she would give it as freely to him as he would to her, so he told her of his love and its obstacle.

'Well, of all the idiotic things I ever heard of,' exclaimed Nettie, 'that beats! Not marry a girl because she is rich; why don't you go into the street and marry a beggar?'

'But Nettie, my honor is at stake,' said poor Joe.

'Honor fiddlesticks! Will honor buy bread and cheese?' said Miss Nettie, with more force than elegance, as she flounced out of the room.

That afternoon Joe received a telegram announcing an intended visit from his friend Bob Wilson. Bob had been his room-mate at the academy and his dearest friend since graduation, and few things could have given him greater pleasure than the promised visit, nor had he long to wait, for in less than an hour 'Breezy Bob,' as we used to call him, burst into the house.

'Well, Joe, how are you, old man?' shouted Bob, as if he were hailing the main topmast-cross-trees in a gale of wind, at the same time giving his friend a blow upon the shoulder that the great John L. would not have blushed for.

Joe returned his greeting more quietly. Bob again threw his arms around his host and hugged him until he fairly gasped.

'I am hugging you now, you dear old hero,' he exclaimed, 'for saving my little sweetheart and her brother; I always said that you were worth all the rest of the Navy put together.'

'Your sweetheart!' faltered Joe. 'Are you engaged to her, then?'

'Well I can't say that there is any formal engage-

6

ment, but it has been an understood thing ever since she was a child, and I should be a cur to go back on it now. Don't you think so?'

'Not unless you loved her, Bob.'

'But suppose she loved me, my dear Joe, as I have every reason to believe she does. Besides, I certainly like her better than any one in the world except you.'

'And so,' thought Joe, 'that the cup of my sorrow may be more bitter, my dearest friend must unconsciously hold it to my lips.'

Nettie, who was a born flirt, began to work her wiles on Bob with such success that he soon discovered that he loved her. This greatly distressed him, for he felt as much bound by honor to marry Annie La Cour as Joe felt bound for the same reason not to. Bob was not the man to shrink from what he thought was right, and with a sad but unflinching heart he fled from the lair of the enchantress and sought the stern path of duty. Arrived at the La Cour's country-seat, with which he was as familiar as any member of the family, he turned into the grove, where he found the object of his search, as he expected, on her favorite rustic seat.

'How are you, Bob,' said she; 'just in time for lunch. Charley has gone to town but father will listen to your stories; only try to moderate your voice, one of the dining-room windows is cracked.'

'Annie,' he said very gravely, 'I have come to say something to you.'

'Well, Master Bob, what is it? I hope you've not been getting into debt.'

'I have come Annie,' and he looked very much as

if he were about to take a pill, 'I have come to ask you to be my wife.'

'What,' long drawn out, '*your* wife. Why Bob Wilson, I suppose I ought to call you Mr. Wilson on this momentous occasion but I can't, we've been brother and sister too long.' Then peal after peal of laughter wakened the echoes of the grove.

'Excuse me, Bob,' said Annie, between her laughs, 'but I can't help it, it is too funny.'

'You don't care for it then,' said Bob, in a tone very unlike that of a despairing lover.

'Why, Bob, you know you do not love me in that way the least bit and I love you quite as little.'

Bob thought it the proper thing to propound a question which his reading had taught him was the usual one on such occasions, so he said: 'May I ask if there is any prior attachment?'

'Now, Master Bob,' said 'Queen Annie', shaking her finger at him 'you got that out of a novel, you know very well you did, and the answer is "None of your business."

Bob now felt so happy at the result of his proposal that he thought to indulge in a little badinage and, simply because Joe Graydon's name was the first that occurred to him, he said, 'Perhaps my friend Graydon may be the happy man.'

The rudeness of the remark could only be excused by his close intimacy with the lady but even that did uot excuse it in this case. Tears sprang to Annie's eyes and her cheeks grew crimson.

'Shame on you,' she cried amid her sobs, 'to insult a poor girl who has always been your friend. You have no right to say such things to me ; leave me I never wish to see you again.'

Bob did not remain long to soothe the angry beauty, but trusting that time would obtain his pardon he hurried back to Long Island on the wings of love more rapidly than he left it on those of duty. Bob, as his late adventure had showed, was not exactly an expert in love matters, but on thinking over matters as he sped over the Hudson River Rail Road he concluded that there was more in his chance question than he had supposed; he duly arrived at his destination where he lost no time in making hay in the light of Miss Nettie's smiles, and as the crop was nearly cured before duty bore him away, in a very few days she had promised to be Mrs. Wilson. Fortunately for the lovers, Joe was in the city that day, so they were not disturbed in the endearments to which engaged people are prone.

After billing and cooing for an hour or two Bob said, 'I wish dear old Joe was in love and as happy as we are.'

'He is in love but I think he does not take it as we do. I'm sure it makes us happy enough, &c. &c. &c.,' which no one has a right to hear or see.

And then from Bob. "But who is he in love with, pet,' 'and why isn't he happy?'

'He's in love with that chit of a girl he took out of a boat and he won't marry her, of all reasons in the world, because she is rich and he is poor. I could understand it if it were the other way.'

'But Nettie, darling, you are going to marry me on my pay.'

'Yes, you dear old boy,' said the practical Nettie, 'but

I would not love you any less if you had a nice little fortune.'

The next day Nettie lunched with a neighbor and the two friends had the house to themselves.

'Joe,' said his friend, 'I have proposed to Annie La Cour.'

'And the result was, I suppose, what you expected.'

'Well, at least it was what I ought to have expected,' answered Bob. 'I was laughed at for a coxcomb, and deserved every bit of it, too. But, Joe, I will tell you a secret. While I was thinking like a fool that I was bound in honor to marry Annie La Cour because she was in love with me I was myself in love with your sister Nettie, who has now promised, with your permission, to be my wife.'

'My dear Bob,' exclaimed Joe heartily, shaking his friend's hand, 'I need not tell you that there is no man on earth to whom I would rather entrust Nettie's future than the friend I have loved and honored for so many years.'

'Now, my dear friend,' continued Bob, 'I have another secret to impart. I have learned that you are attached to Annie La Cour, but restrained by a sense of honor from declaring yourself. Now I can assure you that the obligations of honor are entirely the other way. I discovered in my interview with her that you have won her love and that unless you tell her that she has yours you will allow her to think she has given her love unsought. If you are a gentleman, and I know you are, you will save this poor girl from the sorrow and mortification which she now suffers.

'Save her,' exclaimed Joe, 'I would give my life to save her from a moment's pain or sorrow.'

Bob continued his argument with such good effect that the next morning found Joe setting forth on that mission of which he had so often dreamed, but which, in his waking hours, he had never hoped to accomplish. On his arrival at the La Cour's he inquired for Miss Annie and, on learning that she was in the grounds, he went himself to seek her and found her seated on the same bench that had been the scene of the love, or rather lack-love, passage a few days before.

'Oh, how glad I am to see you,' exclaimed Annie, starting up, and her eyes expressed her delight more eloquently than her words.

'And I am equally glad to see you, Miss La Cour,' said Joe awkwardly, for now that the longed-for moment had arrived,
> 'He feared to put it to the touch.'

'Miss La Cour,' said Annie, reproachfully. 'Has "Queen Annie" been deposed then?'

'No, never,' exclaimed her lover, '"Queen Annie" will reign in my heart forever. Oh, Annie! I have tried so hard to keep it back; honor has warned me that I had no right to ask you to leave this luxury and share poverty with me, but love is the stronger. Annie, dearest Annie, Annie, my queen, I love you. Will you be the wife of one so poor, in all save love, as I?'

'Oh, Joe, dear Joe,' said Annie, as she rested in the arms to which he had clasped her, 'why have you never told me this before and saved me the many tears I have shed because I thought I had given my love unsought.'

The minutes flew, as lover's minutes will, until the unromantic sound of the tea-bell called them to the house. Annie conducted her lover at once to her father, from whom she had never had a secret, and told him the happy news. Mr. La Cour kissed his daughter upon the forehead, and then, taking Joe by the hand, said, in a voice trembling with emotion, ' My young friend, to you, under God, I owe the lives of both of my children ; but for you I should have been a broken-hearted old man in a desolate home. In the course of nature I must soon leave my daughter to the protection of others, and who so fit to shield her from sorrow as you. Take her, my son, and may God in his infinite mercy bless and protect you both.'

Though Joe had returned, as nearly as he could, all the money expended upon him by his uncle, he loved the old man dearly and was deeply grateful for his kindness. He therefore took occasion that very evening to write to him announcing his engagement. On his arrival on Long Island he rather expected an answer to his letter, but was thoroughly surprised, on opening it, to find a cheque for a large amount and the following in his uncle's handwriting and peculiar style :

'MY DEAR JOE :—Glad you're not going to be an old bachelor like your uncle. Marriage is best spite of St. Paul. Of course I'd no idea of keeping your prize-money. Thought young men likely to be improvident, concluded to invest it for you until you needed it. You probably need it now and I am enabled to send you enclosed cheque $3842,31 instead of $3000 you sent me. I have always intended that you should be my heir, but I had to wait for my money until I was too old to enjoy it. I see no good reason why you should. I shall, therefore, give you on your wedding-day a hundred thousand dollars on account of your inheritance. Want a man to look after rents and attend to my business. Give any good man twice what U. S. gives you. War over, no career in navy, better resign and take it. Longest letter I've written in ten years.

' Your affectionate Uncle,

'JOSIAH WILKINS.'

My story is ended, the wedding bells have sounded, 'Queen Annie' has received a crown of happiness, Joe Graydon has accepted his uncle's offer and the navy has lost one of its best and brightest officers."

"A capital story, well told, Mr. Burton, and we are much obliged to you," said the flag-officer, who then turned to the fleet-surgeon, and said,

"Come, doctor, you have been so long in the service, and in so many parts of the world, that you must remember something worthy of note occurring at this season."

"I remember," said the fleet-surgeon, "a frightful gale of wind at Christmas on our own coast, when we were very nearly lost by going to sea against the advice of the pilot; but I fancy we don't want yarns about bad weather to-night. We may have it in reality soon enough, as we are going on the coast in midwinter. My pleasant recollections are all connected with my early service, and therefore rather hazy, while those of the late war are all more or less painful.

"I think I had better read you a love-story written by a young friend of mine. It is much better than anything I could tell you."

Stepping to his state-room, the doctor returned in a moment, and began :

"I have often wondered why it was that a sailor, be he young or old, is so frequently such an irresistible attraction for the fair sex. It may be because 'all the world loves a lover,' and nearly all sailors are lovers, and then again a sailor, a true sailor, is of necessity a brave man, and 'None but the brave deserve the fair.'

These, of course, do not answer the why, and the fact remains that reeling, rolling, rollicking Jack is a great success in winning the admiration of the ladies.

As a rule he is as susceptible as he is successful. The major part of his life being spent outside of the society of ladies, they never become common-place to him; they are ever fresh and attractive to him, and he is naturally lost in admiration of them, when a fair wind puts him in their midst. No sooner does he anchor in a new port than some bright pair of eyes, some soft wavy head of hair, some captivating dimple, some trim figure knocks him off his feet, and he is again, perhaps for the hundredth time, heels over head in love.

The day comes, the hour comes, the woman comes, however, when his manly soul is stirred to its very depths, and then, no matter what his wanderings may be, no matter who may cross his path, no matter what temptations may beset him, ' His heart is true to Polly.' Blown here and there by the winds, carried hither and thither by the currents, tempest-tossed and knocked about on the social sea as well as the salt sea, his heart is as true as his compass-needle.

Lieutenant John George Hartley, or Jack, as he was familiarly called, was one of those large, broad-shouldered, athletic fellows, as strong as an ox, as lithe as a cat; not handsome, but with a heart as big as his body, and a hand-shake that made you realize his ponderous good nature. You felt his whole soul in the palm of his hand, and no one ever grasped his hand that did not become his firm friend. You should have seen him on the deck of a ship to have known his grand character. The sailors worshipped him as a god; yet at times, I must confess, he would seem, to the casual observer, more like a fiend, so intense was he. With perfect control over himself and his men, he was ever master of the situation. He was so honest, sincere and candid in all he did and said that he gained the life-long allegiance of every man with whom he came in contact.

Jack was a great success socially. His quiet dignity and self-possession, his thorough good-heartedness and open frankness, and his fine manly appearance won for him an enviable position. It was but natural that he should have little affairs on hand nearly all the time. He knew, only too well, how to treat all the characters one meets in society. He knew how to amuse the prude, abuse the flirt, and use the tattler.

Jack had a sister whom he worshipped. There was no other woman in the world quite her equal in his estimation, and he seriously doubted if there ever would be. When she returned from a long trip through Europe and Asia Minor, she brought with her many little pieces of stone as souvenirs of her travels. They were chippings from famous buildings, from the pedestals of monuments, from great engineering works; a piece from the Acropolis, a piece from the leaning Tower of Pisa, a piece from Savonarola's fountain, a piece from the Roman aqueduct, a piece from the ruins of Ephesus, and a piece from Mars Hill. These pieces she caused to be ground perfectly flat on both sides and about a sixteenth of an inch in thickness. These flat pieces were then piled one on the other and firmly cemented together. The pile was cut through the centre, making two small composite stones, the cut faces of which represented a cross section of each little piece. These faces were ground and polished, each forming a very pretty striped flat seal for a ring. The ring in which each was mounted was made of three small wires: a gold, a platinum and an aluminum one, braided together.

Having made two of these rings, she gave one to Jack, assuring him that with it she gave a sister's deepest affection, and admonishing him never to part with it, unless he should find some one whom he loved better than himself, and in whom his very life became absorbed. To her he might present it.

It is, perhaps, needless to say that Jack was much affected by this little present, and that he treasured it above all his possessions. He never wore the ring on his finger, but, with a strong silken cord passed through it, he wore it about his neck under his clothing as one does a charm.

The day after we arrived at Villefranche, we, Jack and I, received an invitation to dine with Mrs. Hamnel and her daughter. Although we had planned to spend the afternoon and evening at Monte Carlo, and had made all arrangements so to do, yet we were not long in dropping that plan when we received the invitation to dine at the Hotel D'Angleterre, in Nice. I must confess that my heart jumped when I thought of it, for I was considerably interested in Miss Nita Hamnel, and I had asked myself time and time again in my reveries and musings if I really was in love with her or not. I had had so many little bewilderments and enchantments that I had come to doubt even myself and my own heart.

We left the ship early and arriving at Nice, squandered a little time at the Mediterranean Club, and then went out to stroll on the Promenade des Anglais. On our way to the Promenade we passed the well-known little glove store kept by Madame Garrett. Jack insisted on going in to buy gloves, although I was sure he had twenty pairs of gloves he had already bought here in Nice during the past six months. In we went and we looked over many different shades and styles, and he had tried on a half dozen gloves before he purchased a pair. I noticed that he waited for a certain *demoiselle de magasin* to serve him, and I also noticed a mellow expression of delight, in his large brown eyes, as he rested his elbow on the counter, and she with more patience and care than the case warranted, but with delicate, soothing touch smoothed glove after glove on his generously large hand. This then was one of his little affairs, as he chose to call them. I knew of many another affair, and knowing him as well as I did, I somehow envied the girls on whom he thus smiled.

We were about to leave the store when who should enter but Mrs. and Miss Hamnel. Before he had even exchanged courtesies, I saw that Miss Nita was first startled, then pleased, then fascinated by the expression she had caught on Jack's face. Greetings followed, and hearty ones too, and, as the ladies were out for a short promenade before dinner, they invited us to join them.

It happily fell to my lot to walk with Miss Nita, but we had not gone far before I was sure she was preoccupied with her own thoughts, yet keeping up a lively, joyous conversation with me. Presently she said, 'Lieutenant Hartley seems to have changed somewhat since you all left here in February to go to Tangier.' I replied that I had noticed no change in him, but supposed if there had been any it had come so gradually that a shipmate would not notice it. Here was a pointer, and I began to believe I was not in the race for her affection, or even her interest or consideration.

A most delightful little dinner was served in their apartments, and our hostess was so genial and jolly and entertaining that I began to feel that, perhaps, I was more interested in her than I was in her daughter. Dear friend, remember what old Weller said, and beware of widows. We were sipping pousse cafés and chatting merrily, when, unannounced and with exquisite grace, glided into the room the handsomest man I ever laid eyes upon. Miss Nita welcomed him with a smile, but her face and lips were white as marble, and apparently as hard and cold.

Mrs. Hamnel greeted him with a pleasant word, and we were introdued to Surgeon McElbaine, of the Royal Naval Reserve.

Up to that time our party seemed quite complete, yet he certainly was an addition, for a more polished, refined, witty and entertaining man I had never met. The evening passed all too quickly; we had what one might call a progressive tête-a-tête party, and then Miss Nita and the surgeon sang for us, their voices blending in melodious harmony. Through it all, the color never returned to Miss Nita's face, and I thought her eyes looked sad and sorrowful, wild and bewildered.

Jack did, now, look different from what I had ever seen him before, and, after we returned to the ship that night, we sat up over a bottle of navy sherry and talked it all over for a couple of hours.

As I lay in my bunk, sleepless and nervous, the beads of perspiration on my brow, the cool air from over the water fanning through my air-port, I figured out the result of our deliberations.

Jack was in love with Miss Nita, that was certain, and perhaps she was in love with him.

Jack was jealous of the surgeon, who he had said was a sneaking, snaky scoundrel. He was sure of the latter point, for, when I protested, he insisted that it was written all over his face, that it was in his walk, in his talk, in his finger tips and in his voice.

Miss Nita was the most charming young lady we had ever met.

Mrs. Hamnel, it seemed to me, was a most estimable lady, while to Jack's mind, she was a little queer.

I finally went to sleep, or rather to dream-land, for my sleep was full of visions of the surgeon, Miss Nita, Jack, duels, scenes, love-making bowers, weddings, horrors and ghosts.

Jack went on duty the next day, and I'll warrant it was a long tour of duty to him. I went ashore, and taking advantage of Jack's imprisonment, I paid my respects to the Hamnels.

Miss Nita and I had a cozy little time, and I was getting hopeful of being at least entertaining, when I foolishly introduced the subject of the surgeon. I spoke of how I admired him, but how Jack mistrusted him. With more feeling, energy and fire than I supposed any woman had, she jumped to her feet and said, ' I hate him, despise him, loathe him, but I cannot resist him. Excuse me, please.' She hastily left the room, but as she passed through the portiere she turned and half-smiled, which I took for a sort of an apology for her abruptness.

Mrs. Hamnel explained to me that the surgeon was

one of the most talented and polished gentlemen she had ever met, that he had an occult power that was mysteriously wonderful, and she was very happy that he was interested in Miss Nita. She was sorry that her daughter tried to repulse him, but hoped this childishness, as she termed it, would soon pass away. It was evident to my mind that the surgeon had great power and influence over those two persons, and I began to believe with Jack, that he was not, perhaps, as good as he might be.

Several days later Jack returned on board ship in an excited, troubled state, and taking me into his confidence, told me an incident which caused a cold wave to sweep down my back.

He had had a long talk with Miss Nita, and had declared his deep interest in her, his affection for her, his love to her. Though she did not fully reciprocate, she gave him to understand his address was most pleasing to her, and that she was far from rejecting his suit. Jack's whole heart had gone out to her, and he asked her to accept the stone ring which he carried, after explaining the history and sentiment connected with it. She consented, but insisted on his taking as a guarantee of her liking, fondness and predisposition for him, a small but very fiery opal. She solemnly promised to wear his ring as long as her heart was true to him, and to remove and return it whenever he was dethroned as her suitor and lover.

From the ring they drifted to talking of the reception which was to take place that evening, and to which he was to be her escort. While they were thus chatting, perfectly happy in each other's presence, unannounced again, and this time certainly unwelcomed, entered the surgeon. In his affable manner he declared himself much pleased to see Miss Nita looking so well, and with a hearty, yet hollow laugh, he greeted Lieutenant Hartley. Jack was sorely tempted to knock him down, 'just for luck,' as he said. However, a light and airy conversation was indulged in for a few minutes, in which Mrs. Hamnel soon joined them.

Suddenly Miss Nita, her face ashy white, her eyes sparkling with a few tears that had gone adrift, and her lower lip slightly quivering, said, 'Lieutenant Hartley, it was very kind of you to ask me to go to the reception with you, but I am sorry I shall have to ask you to excuse me. I will have the pleasure of seeing you there, however.' Stunned and bewildered, Jack exclaimed, 'What?' and quietly the sentence was repeated. Beneath the calm exterior a terrible storm of passion, of fright, of hope, of will was raging within Miss Nita.

The surgeon adroitly shifted the conversation, and soon all were apparently in good, animated spirits. Mrs. Hamnel invited both the gentlemen to remain to tea. The surgeon excused himself, alleging that he had a few minor affairs to attend to, and gracefully, courteously, bowed his adieu, and as quietly and noiselessly as he had entered, he passed out through the portiere. Jack remained. Miss Nita gradually calmed and quieted down, and became mistress of herself, and said, 'Lieutenant, I will go with you this evening if, after what has been said, you will take me. You do not know, and I doubt if you can know, what a strain I suffer at times, and how quickly and surely thought travels without visible sign. The surgeon, unknown to you or mamma, made me refuse to go with you, and yet, before he left, he gave his permission. Now don't look at me so, please, please don't, but remain the strong friend you have always been. You don't know what a help you have been to me, my dear Mr. Hartley, in my struggles, and please don't act rashly, or with the vigor your eyes express. It will all be right; I am sure it will, and, to assure you, I will swear now, by this ring, that I shall do all that I can, and I hope to gain strength from this talisman, to rid myself of the despotic power of that man.' Jack in his turn promised that, as long as she wore that ring, he would do whatever she said, as she said, and when she said. He declared himself absolutely and completely at her service, from the broadest matters to the slightest detail. The subject was gradually dropped, and after tea Jack left her, to return a couple of hours later to take her to the reception. She must have been a beautiful sight, as she was dressed for the reception, if Jack's description was at all truthful, and I will warrant that he was the happiest man in the world as he placed her opera cloak around her shoulders and fastened the clasp.

The reception was a most brilliant affair and Miss Nita was second to none in beauty, toilet and pose. She was radiant with charms, and Jack, standing beside her, was in paradise. It was during the second quadrille that the much dreaded pallor came over her again and leaning against her partner, almost fainting, she whispered, 'Jack, my dear Jack, do nothing rash, do nothing without my advice, no matter what happens. You know what I mean. He is here.'

With ball-room floor pitching and tossing like the deck of a ship, with the lights flickering and pulsating, now bright now dark, Jack staggered across the room and soon found himself seated in an easy chair at the door of one of the anterooms. Nita was gone, where, he did not know. He only remembered the smooth politeness of the surgeon, and the 'excuse me, please' of Nita. That was all.

Dazed and bewildered, he took his cloak and left, wandering down the promenade, thence to the Pont Neuf, thence to the Café of the Mason Doré, where he drank and thought, thought, dreamed and drank. Oh shame, that man in his hour of need should appeal to the god who will forsake him, who will betray him. The occupants of the café were growing fewer and fewer, jet after jet was being turned out and he was soon alone, alone with his troubled spirit. The garçon kindly touched him on the shoulder, and asked, 'Does Monsieur wish to retire?' Placing a few francs on the table, Jack left the café and with the aid of the garçon procured a cab. 'Drive anywhere, drive anywhere,' were his orders, but later on, chance brought him, in the early morning, just before break of day, to the Hotel D'Angleterre.

Not knowing why, he wandered up the staircase to the apartments of the Hamnels. All was confusion. Chairs and tables were on their beams ends; trinkets and bric-a-brac were gone; everything was topsy-turvy and not a soul to be seen. Jack, stunned and dumfounded, hardly believing in his own sanity, rushed down stairs to the hotel office and from the clerk, in answer to his queries he learned that the Hamnels had left about midnight, bag and baggage. Where they had gone, no one knew.

Here Jack was, before me, practically a wreck, still

trembling, still agitated. A great, strong, powerful man as weak as a child, a generous, happy soul in the depth of sorrow. I shall never forget him as he sat there on my bunk. I could not comfort him for I knew not how.

That fall he was promoted to be a Lieut. Commander and given command of the gun boat Peoria. He asked me, in fact insisted, on my going with him as executive officer. We were sent to the West Indies and made a complete circuit of the Windward Islands, then drifted off to the more westerly ones. We narrowly missed several heavy cyclones and on September 10th, we anchored off 'Porpoise Key,' near Jamaica. Jack was the same good fellow he had always been and if there was any change in him he had become more tender, less light-hearted, more despondent, less hopeful, more of a cynic, but still a philosopher.

We were walking along the beach and nearing the end of the Key when we saw the wreck of what had been a fine steamer. She had gone pretty well to pieces and was undoubtedly blown ashore during one of the recent gales. Wreckage was to be found all along the beach and some of it was pretty well back from the high tide mark. We sauntered along examining piece after piece but finding nothing of special interest at first. Presently we found the bruised and mangled body of a man. It was a horrible sight, the tropical sun having helped to make it repulsive, but Jack examined it closely. Finding no means of identification further than that the man was probably a Spaniard, he simply remarked, 'We must send some men up here to-morrow and bury this poor fellow.' We continued up the beach and found, first, the body of a child which we moved back further from the water, then the body of a man who, though badly used by the sea, so much resembled our former acquaintance, the sneaking, snaky Surgeon, that I called Jack's attention to it. In the same quiet, cool, calm manner, that characterized him, he examined the body and shreds of clothing and simply said, ' Yes, I am sure it is the Surgeon.'

Jack was a little unnerved, I think, by the thoughts this discovery awoke.

We proceeded, each of us too much occupied with our own thoughts to exchange any, and had gone perhaps a quarter of a mile when we came to the body of a woman. It was, or had been, lashed to a bale of cotton. The rolling of the bale in the heavy surf had pounded and bruised the body and head so that it was impossible to tell what the face must have looked like in life. Quietly, slowly, methodically, Jack examined the clothing and body. He had taken her poor, bruised left hand in his,—a violent shudder shook his whole frame,—he held the hand for me to see,—large crystal tears were in his eyes,—his lips quivered,—on his face was the saddest expression I had ever seen,—a picture of deep, racking, hopeless, profound sorrow. There, on her finger, was Jack's ring.

How the thoughts ran riot through my brain. I seemed burning with excitement and chilled with horror. Ah, well, then Miss Nita had been true to Jack all this time. Whatever else she had done, wherever she had been, she had been loyal, even to the last moment of her life, to her most worthy lover, Jack. I believed in the truth of the ring and its sentimental significance.

Around the mound of Nita's grave were placed King and Queen conchs, and the head-stone consists of a large white-winged piece of coral. A bayonet marks the surgeon's grave.

Tenderly restoring the opal ring to her finger, Jack took and kept his stone ring, and I often thought how much it now meant to him.

Poor, dear fellow, how I pitied him, how my heart suffered for and with him.

No, my story is not ended.

It was two months later, long dreary months they were, too, that, arriving at Havana, Jack received in the mail a letter which he showed me.

> MY DEAR JACK:—I am coming to you now. By the goodly help of the ring you gave me, I am coming to you with a pure heart and free hand. The world is so bright to me now. Have you kept the opal, and has it kept you mine? The steamer leaves at five for St. Thomas, where I hope to find you, but, if I do not, I shall follow on, for I intend to follow you to the end of the earth. Surely your ring will not fail me now, it will and it must lead me to you. With a heart full of love and hope.
>
> Your own, true,
> NITA.

This seemed the last straw. How terrible this all was and how I did admire Jack. How any man could stand the strains to which he had been subjected, how anything less than a god could do it, was beyond my knowing. It was evident she had lost her life in searching for her lover, when hopes were highest, when she had so much to live for.

The day before we left Havana, an English tramp steamer arrived from Trinidad, and, that afternoon, I had the pleasure of escorting to the cabin and announcing to Jack, Miss Nita Hamnel.

You may doubt the existence of a heaven in the next world, if you will, but some people have found heaven in this. The scene that I witnessed was far too sacred for me to profane with an attempt at description.

* * * * * * * *

The surgeon had prevailed upon Mrs. Hamnel and her daughter to leave Nice, and had carefully avoided leaving a trace as to where they had gone. He no doubt feared Jack. He had had a fac-simile of Jack's ring made because he had admired it, and was unable to persuade Miss Nita to give it to him. Through the kindly influence of the ring, Miss Nita had been enabled to gradually extricate herself from the control of the surgeon. He, finding his power over her waning, reluctantly gave her up. The last Miss Nita knew of him he had eloped with the weak but handsome wife of a wealthy old miller. Poor Mrs. Hamnel had died at Florence, Italy, of fever, and, after recovering from the fatigue of caring for her mother and the shock her death caused, Miss Nita set out to find Jack.

* * * * * * * *

Commander John George Hartley and Miss Nita Hamnel were married at the house of Mrs. Neilson Upton Butterworth, sister of Commander Hartley.

I believe in the power of amulets, the fidelity of woman's love, the grand possibilities of man's character, and a heaven on earth."

A silence, followed by a murmur of applause, followed Mr. Digit's story, and then the steward filled the glasses for the last time.

The "Amulet" was voted a great success, although some of the younger men giggled a little at the reader, whom they had not associated with such a story, even as its reader.

Then the Doctor, "having the call," looked along the table, and said: "I think we will all like to hear from Mr. Hawse, who won't give a love story, I am sure."

Mr. Hawse, the gentleman referred to, was sitting near the end of the table—a curly-haired, blue-eyed man, with an alert manner and good-humored expression which made him the favorite of every one on board, from the flag-officer to the captain of the head. He was the sort of man a ship's company will always work for without driving; his two expressions when carrying on duty being, "Cheerily, men!" and "Handsomely! handsomely, lads!" and he had to use the last most frequently, to keep from springing something.

Coming from a respectable New England family, some of whom, in each generation, had been sailors, he had, previous to the late war, been mate of an Indiaman. Entering the service as an acting master, he had, by good conduct and hard fighting, as well as ability as a navigator, attained the rank of lieutenant in the regular navy. Still a young man, and proud of his success, when so many had failed, he never forgot the service from which he had sprung; so that, while not a great talker, he occasionally held forth upon the achievements of our merchant sailors in all parts of the world; and was, besides, a perfect encyclopedia of the great ocean routes, prevailing winds and currents, and of rapid passages under sail. He always deprecated the prejudices which exist, more or less, between the navy and the merchant service, and was wont to say that they were nearer to each other, and more essential to each other, than either would admit. In fact, Mr. Hawse maintained, with great ability and perfect truth, that they were only specialties of the same profession.

In illustration of the material, for officers alone, derived from the merchant service during the late war, he said:

"I do not adduce the many able merchant captains and mates who, as acting officers of the navy, reflected credit upon it and upon themselves, but I will tell you of an ordinary seaman (entirely illiterate, though a Yankee, born and bred) who became an officer, and sustained his position without discredit until honorably discharged at the close of the war.

It was during the 'Burnside Expedition' that I first saw the man of whom I speak. During this expedition—one of the first 'joint,' or combined ones of the war—the army and navy had very mixed duties, and the lines of distinction between soldier and sailor were not very closely drawn,—but no matter about that. The rendezvous of the expedition was Hatteras Inlet, where the vessels began to assemble in the latter days of 1861.

The gunboat to which I was attached was early upon the scene, and, one by one, during the stormy Christmas week, and all the January following, reinforcements came in, now in the shape of an East River ferry-boat, with heavy nine-inch guns mounted on either end, and now a yacht, with the gentleman owner in command; and now again, a transport, with troops, stores, or munitions of war,—the latter generally requiring our aid to pull them over the outer bar. Not all of them, despite our care, got in safely. Several were wrecked, with great loss of important stores and not a few lives. After a time, however, all that were expected arrived at the rendezvous, and soldiers and sailors then moved harmoniously to their appointed work.

In the early part of February, 1862, we advanced upon Roanoke Island, and soon drove behind the works; we were to attack Commodore Lynch, of the Confederate navy, which gentleman had been using us as a target for the past month of preparation without much reply upon our part. After a long day's battle the works surrendered, with their garrison of three thousand men, and it was during that day's fight that I had occasion to notice the ordinary seaman of whom I spoke. Ephraim Boomer, as he signed himself four years after that, or E. $\overset{\text{his}}{\times}$ Boomer, as it was signed for him in the shipping register in Boston, a few months before, was the person in question. His 'descriptive list' might run as follows:

'Place of birth, Massachusetts; age, twenty; occupation, the sea; complexion, fair; height, five feet ten inches; eyes, dark; hair, brown. Marks or scars: Hope, with foul anchor, on left forearm, in Indian ink; no colors; no scars. To serve three years, unless sooner discharged.'

This would pretty well describe our gallant young sailor on the 7th of February, 1862. On the next day he had earned the position of an officer, and this is how it came about:

Our present Vice-Admiral Rowan, then a commander, in organizing the Flotilla of the Sounds, under Admiral Goldsborough, turned a little coasting sloop, called the 'Granite,' into a magazine; her business being to keep out of harm's way, and yet convenient enough to supply the gunboats with ammunition when they had exhausted the first supply in their small magazines. Of course every officer begged to be excused from taking charge of the *Granite*, as in her there appeared to be no chance of distinction in the coming fight. And so it finally happened, in the stress of affairs, that the young, fresh-looking, intelligent Yankee boy, who had been working fore-and-afters round Cape Cod all his life, and thoroughly understood them, was actually left in this important charge, with stringent orders to work up to a position, but to keep out of fire.

On the morning of the battle, after the fight had raged hotly for three or four hours, the gunboat to which I was attached obtained permission, by signal, to temporarily withdraw and run down to the magazine, for the purpose of replenishing her exhausted ammunition. While alongside we put on board the sloop a small pop-gun of a cannon which we had captured some time before, and which we found only to encumber our decks while engaged with the works. The fire was so hot, and lasted so long, that by the afternoon the magazine had been visited by almost all the vessels, and then forgotten, when, close in under the land (closer than any of us could go on account of the shoal water), was seen a small sailing-vessel hotly engaged with a battery of the enemy. She was soon recognized, to our horror, as the sloop *Granite*,—the *magazine*,—and E. Boomer was distinctly seen, with his four men, coolly serving our discarded small piece.

Of course E. Boomer was next morning formally reported as guilty of gross disobedience of orders in the face of the enemy. But, in the mean time, we had gained a victory, and our flag-officer, Goldsborough, intimated to the reporting officer that he could afford to be lenient toward those who had only erred through excess of zeal and courage. Indeed, upon consideration, he determined that we wanted just such men at that time, and E. Boomer's pluck was allowed to entirely overbalance his disobedience of orders, and he was recommended for an appointment.

The Navy Department being at that time fully alive to the policy of stimulating the youthful American naval mind, acted promptly on the flag-officer's recommendation, and Boomer mounted his shoulder-straps in a very few days, and was respected and heartily obeyed during the whole war. I may say, moreover, that he learned to read and write, and a good deal more than that, before he was honorably discharged; and wherever he may be now, I know that he is worthily upholding the character of a Yankee sailor."

"You must have had more than the usual number of curious characters in that improvised 'Flotilla of the Sounds,' Mr. Hawse," said the admiral, knocking the ashes from his cigar and taking a sip of Madeira.

"Yes, indeed! Plenty of them, sir!" said Hawse; "but the other one that I remember best was David Davis."

"David Davis!—Davis! Wasn't he the fellow in the magazine that Aleck M—— used to tell the yarn about?"

"Yes, sir! the very man! I think there is no record of this hero in the Navy Department at all; and yet he was more entitled to honorable mention than many who received it. Few indeed during the whole war performed an act of such signal gallantry.

David Davis had been a merchant seaman all his life, and at the time I speak of was past middle age. He was very square-built, especially that part of him which in a sailor is supposed to be small and snug. In fact, D. D. was built like a Dutch galliot, very full in the counter. Being too heavy to move easily aloft, or even about the deck, his commanding officer—poor Chaplin, of the *Valley City*—made him a gunner, and he was stationed in the magazine, of course, in time of action. This magazine in the purchased gunboat was a curious arrangement, and very much exposed. It was simply a large box hung under the deck, and extending, about amidships, clean across the little vessel. Divided into two parts, the powder, in large cartridges, was stowed on one side, and the blue-lights, rockets, Coston's signals, and other pyrotechny were on the other.

During the short but terribly severe little fight at Elizabeth (the one which brought Rowan to the front, and eventually made him vice-admiral, as he deserved), our friend David was at his post, cool and imperturbable, filling boxes and passing powder for the big gun, when a shell from a Confederate gunboat passed through both parts of the magazine, exploding in and setting fire to that part which contained the blue-lights and other combustibles. If the shell had not made a big hole in the bulkhead between the two parts there would have been but little comparative urgent danger. But in the actual position of affairs—with sparks and spits of fire flying freely, and not confining themselves to their own compartment—David Davis may be said to have been in a 'fix.' He was equal to the occasion, however. Instead of jumping on deck to report damages and leaving the magazine to blow up, he, with pluck, presence of mind, and perfect reliance upon his personal qualities, promptly placed the broadest part of his person against the hole in the bulkhead, and held it there firmly, so as to arrest the shower of sparks.

Of course, with the noise of guns and the excitement on deck, they were totally ignorant of what had occurred in the magazine, and soon all hands, from captain to powder-boy, were cursing David for not passing powder. At last, as no boxes were produced by objurgation, an officer was sent below to find out the reason. Then the truth came out; but D. Davis still stuck to his post until the fire division with their hose had relieved him of care.

D. Davis had to be put under the surgeon's care, for his injuries were quite painful. All on board felt that their lives had probably been saved by his coolness and courage, although these qualities had been exhibited in such an extraordinary way, and for this act he was recommended to the Department for an appointment as acting master. At his own urgent request, however, the letter was canceled, so that he might not be restricted from his favorite pleasure—getting drunk on liberty."

"It's well the man Davis was so big in those parts," solemnly remarked the captain, when Mr. Hawse had finished his yarn.

"Humph!" added the admiral. "I hope his commanding officer gave him a new pair of breeches."

"Sailors are queer creatures," continued the admiral. "I remember hearing old Captain McC—— relate how, when he, as first lieutenant of the *Enterprise*, boarded and captured the English *Boxer*, he found an old 'shell-back' of the English ship carefully stowing away a bundle wrapped in canvas.

'What have you there, my lad?' said McC——, having visions of bullion being secreted.

'Pig-tail, to keep from the d—d Yankees?' replied the unterrified son of Albion to his captor.

Tobacco was then, to the English, very precious, while to our people, in consequence of the blockade, it was a mere drug; and the busy way of the queer old fellow over a trifle, at such a time as that, struck McC——'s fancy, and he had the old fellow looked out for, and saw that he had his grog.

" Poor old McC——," continued the admiral, with his eyes cast up retrospectively at the beams; "they used to tell a story about him that, at the court-martial of an officer for drunkenness, in the old three-bottle days, he was summoned as a witness, and asked whether he had ever seen the accused drunk.

'Yes,' said McC——; 'yes, gentlemanly drunk, as I have seen *all* this honorable court.'

As may be supposed, the Judge-Advocate did not pursue McC——'s examination very much further."

" By George, Mr. Hawse!" continued the flag-officer, who was by this time enjoying himself thoroughly, " I am tempted to cap your story of David Davis by another, which, though perhaps not very refined, is equally true, and resulted in the saving of a good ship and many lives. It happened thus:

" About twenty-five years ago, during the winter sea-

THE FLAG-OFFICER'S STORY. 111

son, the steamer *Persia*, of the Cunard line, arrived in New York from Liverpool upon her first trip. She was a new vessel, modeled and built for speed as well as strength, and intended to compete with the time which the vessels of the famous Collins line of American steamers were making in their passages over the Atlantic.

One of the steamships of this Collins line had been advertised to leave Liverpool at or near the same hour as the Cunarder mentioned, and heavy bets had been made as to which of these vessels would make the quickest passage, opinions differing in every case in accordance with the nationality of the persons interested. As several days elapsed after the arrival of the *Persia* with no appearance of the American ship, the chagrin which her backers felt gave place to a fear lest an accident of grave import should have happened. The feeling intensified as vessels arriving about this period reported falling in with heavy field-ice, and also as having seen bergs far to the southward of the latitude in which they are usually met with. It likewise became known that the *Persia* had, on her passage, ran into a small berg or heavy field-ice, and that in this collision her bow-plates were crushed to a considerable extent, from which damage, but for the fact of having been built with compartments, she would in all probability have gone to the bottom.

Under these circumstances, prominent citizens of New York requested the Navy Department to send a vessel in search of the missing steamer. The only available one the Department had at this time was the little steamer *Arctic*, then lying at the Brooklyn Navy Yard, and she was promptly placed at the disposal of the applicants, and the navy-yard authorities were directed to get her in readiness with all dispatch. This vessel had returned from a cruise in the Polar regions only a short time before, having been cruising there in search of Dr. Kane's expeditionary party. Originally intended for use as a light-ship, to be anchored on the 'Sow and Pigs' shoal, her hull had been constructed with great strength, to enable it to withstand the heavy seas that are always raised on those shoals by the violent gales of winter. Owing to this strength of build she had been selected, while yet on the stocks, by the officer who was to command the Polar party, as being the most suitable vessel he could find for the service on which he was to be sent, and as one which, with some alterations, would have the requisite strength to resist any ice-squeezes she might have to undergo during the cruise in those northern latitudes.

The Navy Department had therefore, on his suggestion, purchased the vessel and altered her into a steamer, with a small auxiliary engine and propeller, having power enough, in perfectly smooth water, to give a speed of four knots. She was rigged as a brigantine, and under sail could make eight knots if the wind and sea were favorable. Owing to the weight of boiler, engine and coal, when stowed for sea, she trimmed very much by the stern, so much so, in fact, that while aft her deck was not more than four feet clear of the water, forward it was at least seven feet. From this description it will readily be perceived that the *Arctic* was in no respect fitted to be a cruiser or capable of rendering aid to any vessel needing it during bad weather. She was an odd-looking craft,—

'And, taking *her* all in all,
We ne'er shall look upon her like again.'

A volunteer crew of five officers and forty men was soon made up from those on board the receiving-ship *North Carolina*, and while they were hurriedly getting their traps together for this sudden departure, the navy-yard authorities were as hurriedly preparing the vessel for sea. After stowing her full of coal, provisions, and stores, they filled her spar-deck, or rather the waist, with lumber even with the rail: for what purpose this was to be used not one of us on board could imagine, and even to this day I have been unable to find out. Perhaps it was for building rafts or in lieu of life-preservers. In a few hours everything was in readiness, and we steamed away from the yard amid the cheers of at least a thousand persons who had assembled on the docks to see the little craft depart upon her errand of mercy.

Early in the evening we arrived outside the bar, discharged the pilot, and stood to the eastward, with a light southerly wind, clear weather, and sea as smooth as a mill-pond. During the first twenty-four hours our time was fully occupied in finding where things were stowed, in putting them to rights, and getting into a ship-shape condition. We found a number of boxes filled with fresh provisions packed in ice, sufficient in quantity to last a year's cruise, the friends who had sent these contributions to our larder evidently determining that our 'inner man' should not suffer, no matter what hardships the outer man might have to undergo. These friends had also provided a cook, who, if appearances indicated anything, indicated good living, for he weighed at the least three hundred pounds; in stature he was about five feet.

These solid qualifications proved eventually to be of the greatest importance.

On the second day the wind freshened, and banking fires, we trusted entirely to the sails; but as the wind increased in force so did the sea in height, and an occasional comber breaking over the rail proved to us that the *Arctic* was not to be much of a sea-boat in case really bad weather should be encountered. Shortly after the sea had commenced to break on board a leak was reported, the water entering the fire-room through the port coal-bunker; it did not amount to much, as the occasional use of the 'donkey-pump,' running at half speed, served to keep the water down. As the day wore on the wind gradually increased in force until it became a gale, with a heavy sea accompanying, and by night it was blowing a hurricane from the south-southeast, and the rain descending in torrents. We had shortened sail as required from time to time, until we were 'lying-to' under a close-reefed foretopsail and balance-reefed mainsail. The leak by this time had certainly become troublesome, if not dangerous, requiring the donkey-pump to be run continuously at full speed, and this barely served to keep the water from rising over the fire-room floor. With much labor we managed to secure a sail with heavy mats outside the hull, over that position where the leak was supposed to be; but it was of no use, for the water still continued to pour into the fire-room through the port coal-bunker.

Knowing that southeasters upon our coast are short-lived, winding up with heavy rain and then with a sudden shift of wind to the northward and westward, we wore ship, and kept a bright lookout for the expected change.

THE FLAG-OFFICER'S STORY. 115

It came at midnight,—due northwest and butt-end foremost,—bringing bitterly cold weather along with it, which, very shortly, coated everything above hatches with ice. The sea, from the shift of wind, became very irregular, breaking on board at all points, from aft as well as forward, with almost a continual swash from either side.

As the water came on board so did the leak increase, and the donkey-pump not being capable of freeing us, we were obliged to hook the 'bilge-injection.' We then prepared the boats for lowering, placing a bag of bread and a bundle of blankets in each, it being, in the opinion of the officers, only a question of time—and that not a very distant period—before the vessel must go down. These boats were two in number, and large enough to hold all hands in case nothing was placed in them in addition to the bread and blankets mentioned. We determined, however, to stick to the ship until the last moment that we possibly could, as it was very doubtful if boats could live in such a sea, and if they did, it was still more doubtful whether any one in an open boat could survive the intense cold. So we bailed as well as pumped, anxiously looking for daylight.

The weather at this time was clear, the barometer very low, rising slowly, if at all, this indicating that the gale would be of long continuance. As the sea became more regular it did not break on board so frequently, and our hopes were correspondingly increased. Suddenly a green sea curled over the bows, flooding the decks; the leak increased, the fires were extinguished, and the engine, with one long-drawn sigh, ceased to work, and the *Arctic*, with ten feet of water in her engine-room, but with not one drop forward, was sinking, going down stern foremost. A rush was made by the crew for the boats; but the stern voice of command was heard above the din of the elements, 'Be quiet, men! Mr. Bluegrass, take charge of the port boat. I will take charge of the starboard. Now, starboard watch, starboard side; port watch, port side. Clear the decks! throw everything overboard! Work with a will, men; work for your lives!'

They did so, and in an incredibly short space of time the decks were cleared, both the wind and the sea seeming to aid us in our struggle for existence, as the one lulled temporarily and the other ceased to break on board. When the last plank of the deck-load of lumber was thrown clear of the side, the cause of all our trouble was plainly in view. The source of the leak was apparent. *A coal-bunker plate had been left off*, and was not on board, and careless workmen at the navy-yard had stowed lumber *over the hole*. Consequently, every drop of water that came upon the decks went below through the open bunker down to the vitals of the ship. My action was taken instantly, for should another sea roll over us, or a swash merely come on board before that bunker was closed, sink we must.

'COOK, SIT ON THAT HOLE!!'

He did so, covering the aperture completely! The leak was stopped! Fortunate for us that it was, for scarcely had he taken his seat ere another green sea tumbled over the rail, deluging our decks; but our cook sat firm, and ocean's proud waves were stayed effectually from ingress to the depths of the vessel. I protected the fat man from the water and the weather as much as possible, covering him with blankets, and at daylight relieved him from that uncomfortable position, sealing the bunker with tarred canvas and sheet lead.

> 'Imperial Cæsar, dead and turned to clay,
> Might stop a hole to keep the wind away;'
> But our great cook, though no imperial lout,
> Did stop a hole, and keep the water out.'

We bailed all night and until noon of the day, and, as no more water came into the vessel's hold, every drop we discharged told. Having lowered it sufficiently, we started fires, and steam soon freed us from all that remained, and the *Arctic* was 'as tight as a bottle.'

For three days the gale continued, during which time we were compelled to 'lie to,' all hands being as uncomfortable as can well be imagined, the decks being continually under water. When it moderated we made sail and stood to the eastward, keeping as near to the track taken by ocean steamers as possible. Occasionally we met and spoke a vessel, but could learn nothing from them in regard to the missing steamer.

When we arrived off Sable Island the weather was fine, so standing in to the northwestern end, we anchored, and sent a boat on shore to inquire if aught had been heard in regard to her. As this island is in the track of vessels bound to and from Europe, it was decided to examine the shores thoroughly, as many vessels have been lost thereon. We did so, but could see nothing lately wrecked. Then we stood to the eastward and cruised. Days passed, weeks passed, and still we cruised; finally giving up all search as hopeless, we turned the vessel's head westward, and arrived back at the navy-yard after an absence of nearly two months.

I may add that the steamer *Pacific*, of the Collins line, never was heard of after her departure from Liverpool. Her fate is one of the secrets of the great sea.

Conversation now naturally turned to that fruitful source of speculation among all sailors, the probable fate of the transatlantic steamers which have from time to time disappeared, without leaving a trace behind them. From those thus engaged must be excepted Mr. Gasket and a select group of two or three in his immediate neighborhood, to whom that lively lieutenant was reciting (*sotto voce*, and apropos of the flag-officer's story of the lumber on the deck of the *Arctic*) the old coaster's answer (when hailed, in distress, in the Gulf Stream),—

> ' My name is John Turner,
> I'm master and owner
> Of the high-deck-éd schooner
> Called the Julian-ner,
> Bound from North-Carliner
> To Bërmūder,
> With a deck-load o' staves
> And a hold full o' lumber.'

"When requested to send his boat for supplies." said Gasket, "he merely finished with,—

> ' My long-boat is stove,
> And I h'aint got no other ! '

and all the time the poor fellow was not conscious that he was dropping into rhyme, however halting."

After a little private giggle over the quaint jingle, Gasket said, " Let's draw out the young doctor. I never heard him tell a story, and I never heard him laugh. Now's the time or never."

The " doctor " referred to was the passed assistant

surgeon, a man much more devoted to microscopy, photography and botany than to telling yarns. Not at all a bad fellow, ready and willing to do a good turn or to take a part in any general action of the mess, he still principally preferred to be let alone to pursue his own favorite studies.

Being called upon, the doctor, to the surprise of all, and especially of Gasket and his set, who had never been able to make anything of him, actually began to talk as if he intended to keep it up.

"I think I remember no very striking event at Christmas," said the doctor, "but I did spend one anniversary of the day, three or four years ago, almost alone, and amid as glorious scenery and surroundings as the earth can produce. If you don't mind I will try to recall the day."

"Go on, doctor!" said the flag-officer, with whom the quiet, saturnine medical officer was a prime favorite, perhaps from the mere doctrine of opposites.

"We were in the brig *Plunger*," said the doctor, "and lying at St. Catherine's, on the coast of Brazil, —a favorite resort of our vessels then. It was a great place for fishing, especially with the seine, and the men used to enjoy it extremely. We also used to get lots of native, or 'raccoon' oysters, about as big as a dollar, which tasted remarkably well to those who had had none of those bivalves for a year or two. On the occasion I speak of the mess was to have a dinner and general Christmas jollification, which promised to be pretty heavy, and I had a special reason to avoid anything of the kind just then, having within a day or two received news of the death of a near and dear relative. So I determined to pass the day in a long ramble over the island, and the evening with a friend on board one of the other ships of the squadron, not returning to our brig until everything was settled for the night.

As most of you know, Saint Catherine's is an island, and yet so near the mainland as to fully share its wonderful flora and fauna; so situated as to enjoy many of the pleasures of the tropics while escaping some of its pains; without a regular rainy season, yet having showers equal to any under the line; just beyond the Tropic of Capricorn; with fresh and irregular breezes; with lovely and diversified scenery, and a climate which makes it a selected point for *poitrinaires* in that empire. One would suppose, from such a description, that Santa Catherina was a paradise upon earth. And so it would be if certain reptiles and insects, and other drawbacks, inseparable from this lower sphere, were absent.

The name of the capital town of the island, which is also the capital of a small province of Brazil, is certainly not a promising one, being 'Nossa Senhora do Desterro,' —*Our Lady of Banishment.* Yet the foreigners who have lived there come to like it as a residence, while the natives look upon it as the centre of all comfort, delight, and joy.

It was raining as I started in the early morning for a day's ramble over the island, but I did not mind that, for it rained more or less every day, and I knew it would hold up and be lovely weather in an hour or two.

Being put on shore from the ship at one of the sandy

bights within view, my first discovery on foreign soil was a huge pile of anthracite coal, stored upon a flat ledge of rock a few feet above the water, which might have led me to suppose myself in Pennsylvania if I had not strong evidence to the contrary in the surrounding scene. This coal, I was told, belonged to the United States government.

At the sandy cove, the termination of a quebrada, a small stream came down from the mountain, and some houses were snuggled away among bananas and plantains, dwarf palms and orange-trees. The houses were of one story, of quite solid masonry, washed with bright blue, yellow, or white, and with window-casings and doors of some violently-contrasting colors. The roofs were generally of heavy red tiles, and this being a village of quite well-to-do people, many had iron gratings or bars in their windows.

A large number of cur dogs met me, and welcomed me with barks and snarls, until some negroes, who were hanging about, came to my assistance and drove them away. Real negroes, these! without any pretense to be anything else,—with tufted heads and great prognathous jaws, with woolen caps and clay-colored shirts and breeches of a coarse material, made on purpose for slave wear, and almost as distinctive a badge of their condition as is the striped suit of a jail-bird that of his. I saw no white people,—indeed, few purely white were there. There was one shop,—the principal wares in which seemed to be potable ones,—presided over by a bright mulatto dame, of about two hundred pounds weight, in a brilliant, short, striped petticoat, white chemise, thrown well off one shoulder, and a long cigar in her mouth.

In one of the houses, the door of which was open, were evidences of civilization, in the shape of an argand lamp and some illustrated newspapers, as well as a rocking-chair. I made out that this establishment belonged to an American, long a resident of the island, who was also the owner of a plantation to the southward. He sometimes came here to sell fruit and vegetables to whalers or men-of-war, and also had charge of the little mountain of coal, which I had seen near the landing. The whole of the mongrel population was for the moment absorbed in the slaughtering of two half-wild beeves, which had been driven down from the hills to the beach and there shot, to afford a supply of fresh beef to the few ships in the bay. Although my Portuguese was deficient, I found that I made out better here than in more civilized localities,—gestures going a long way,—and, approaching the little crowd surrounding the butchers, I was not long in engaging a remarkably monkified old negro to accompany me for the day as a guide. Although he looked excessively like a gray-haired baboon, I found him intelligent in his way, and, after he had secured his share of the *tripas*, or offal, of the slaughtered cattle and confided it to the care of a small boy who looked exactly like him, we started up the hill-side by a well-beaten but narrow path.

By the time we had ascended about fifty feet above the water we came upon a little plateau, which contained the graves of most of the foreigners who had died on board ship here for years past. Among others were those of two young sisters, daughters of General S——, who was formerly governor of Washington Territory, and the same who met his death at Chantilly during the late war. He was on his way out to his post, by sailing-ship,—the only mode of proceeding at that period,—and, calling at Rio, they contracted yellow fever, of which these poor girls died, after the arrival of the ship at Desterro, in distress. I was told that an inscription on copper had been placed over their grave, but the material proved an irresistible temptation to the half-civilized neighbors, and it was carried off; as was another plate placed there by one of our men-of-war. I believe a more permanent monument has been placed there since my visit.

The spot, though neglected, was naturally a lovely one, inclosed by dense vegetation, but still affording glimpses of the blue waters of the bay. The surrounding bush was overrun with wild vanilla, which has a most graceful twining stem, a pretty leaf, and a profusion of star-shaped flowers. As it does not produce the bean of commerce the people do not disturb it.

After showing me this peaceful spot my guide insisted, in a queer sort of way, upon my following him to a neighboring ravine, where he made me understand most of the slaves were buried in a pit, apparently chuckling over the idea that the white strangers and his own people were equally excluded from consecrated ground.

Passing upwards and inland, we found bananas and dwarf palms in the little valleys, while the ridges were mostly occupied either by the virgin forest or by coffee-trees, some in cultivation and some far beyond that, for no colt runs wild sooner than a coffee-tree. Negroes, with heavy hoes and machetes, were working among the young trees, plantations of which ran up the hills on all sides in clearings made in the forest.

The coffee-plant requires constant and tender care. Farther north, within the tropic, it (like the cacao) flourishes best in the shade of other trees, but in this favored clime it stands forth by itself and takes the sun. It must be carefully weeded during its early growth,—no small labor in such a climate and soil,—and it is seldom allowed to grow to more than ten or twelve feet in height if the cultivator is a careful one, but in abandoned plantations, it straggles up to three times that height. They bear from three years old, and their useful life is about twenty years. The bloom is beautiful and very odorous, but short-lived, and the berry, when ripe, is of the size and color of a large cranberry. The harvest is usually made three times a year, when the hull is pounded off, and the grains, as we know them, spread out every day on the *terreno*, or terrace,—a spot in full sunshine all day long, paved and coped with dressed stone, or sometimes laid in cement. Here the drying and picking goes on at the hands of women and children, or of old and disabled men. A sharp owner or overseer hovers about these with a bright lookout for showers, so as to have the coffee under cover in time.

Orange plantations were common, but small in extent, for the fruit grows so finely that almost everyone has his own trees,—the only outside demand being from an occasional whaler or some chance man-of-war.

In most suitable localities the mandioc was growing, —*Jatropha manihot*,—about the most important Brazilian staple, as, with the great mass of the people, it takes the place of wheat flour. It is not an easy plant to cultivate, requiring not only care and labor, but patience, for it takes from twelve to eighteen months to come to maturity, and during that time it has to be gone over twelve or fifteen times with the heavy hoe to prevent its shoots from being crowded out of existence by its more lush tropical and semi-tropical neighbors,—one can hardly call them weeds. But the plant is worth the labor, for it produces six times as much food to the acre as the best wheat. The root is in appearance not unlike a parsnip. Its preparation is one of the most important operations of South American domestic economy, quite as much so as milling with us. But the private maker has the advantage here,—that his preparation is better than that made upon a large scale and for sale. The mandioc trough, grater, and curiously plated bag of grass-fibre for pressing out the juice form a part of the utensils of every country establishment, large or small. The roots are boiled, and the rind then removed, after which they are grated on a huge grater, the fragments falling into a trough dug out of hard wood, which is bestraddled by the operator. The mass is then collected from the trough, and squeezed in the long bag until all the juice is expressed, this being very poisonous. It is then thoroughly beaten in large iron-wood mortars, with long and heavy pestles, and, as a final operation, it is dried over the embers in shallow pans. The product is a coarse but very white powder. The juice deposits, upon standing, a fine substance, which, after treatment, becomes tapioca, and is sent to form sick diet and to make bad puddings all over the world. There is another kind of mandioc, called aipim, which is not poisonous. It is simply roasted like a potato or plantain, but it is by no means so much valued as the other variety.

Beside the staple I have just described, a good deal

of maize is raised, which is used in much the same way as in our Southern States. There is great variety in the color of the grain, as, in addition to the usual rich yellow, pure white, black, red and violet ears are seen hanging in bundles from the beams and rafters of the huts, and forming about the only ornament of many of them.

Passing beyond the plantations we surmounted a ridge six or seven hundred feet high, and then began to descend toward the centre of the island, which is nearly surrounded by this mountainous rim. The central portion contains a lake of some size, the home of the ibis, with plumage of most delicate pink and crimson, as well as of myriads of water-fowl. Huge herons and cranes of lovely colors—snowy-white, stone-blue, or gray and pink—are also common, as are plovers of several varieties. Black-necked geese and ducks innumerable rose from the small ponds and marshes as we disturbed them, and made toward the great lake; while soaring high over all, like spots in the clear blue sky, were the carácarás, or vulture eagles, ready to pounce upon any maimed beast or solitary bird, or to devour any carrion. The lake is surrounded by a rich rolling country, not only beautiful, but remarkable for the fact that almost anything will grow there, either of the tropic or temperate zone. There was, however, but little cultivation, and the eye ranged over forests alternating with savannas, the first containing trees of great size and beauty, many of them loaded with bloom, and bearing, in addition, quantities of parasites in the form of orchids. Almost every trunk and branch supported some of these, in addition to convolvuli of surprising growth and grace. On the edge of the savannas, bignonias flourished, charming masses of color, and the passion-flower emulated the convolvulus in vigor of growth and bloom.

Anything more gloriously beautiful and wonderfully varied than the orchids cannot be found, and although now so common in the conservatories, especially in England, no transplantation to Kew or Chatsworth can give one a proper idea of them,—their gorgeous colors, rare odor, and prodigious variety,—as seen in this belt of country, where they are nourished by the constant moisture and semi-tropical sun. These air-plants are the more curious from the frequent imitation of the forms of butterflies, birds, and insects, although, perhaps, we should put it the other way, and say, with Darwin, that the birds and insects imitated the flowers. There is one orchid flower which is held in high estimation and honor among the natives,—the 'Flor do Espiritu Santo.' It is the perfect representation of a white dove descending, with a background of lovely rich-colored petals. The 'air-plants,' if removed with any care at all, will live for weeks and months on board ship, and the wonder is that more are not brought to our country, and houses built for them where they can have the requisite heat and moisture combined.

Beside these glorious creations we found, in the deeper forest, ferns which seemed to emulate in growth the trees which bore the orchids, while every rock and trunk and stem afforded curious lichens and mosses.

In these deeper woods are no flowers or birds, and few insects,—there is too much shade for them,—but in the little *campos* to which we came, now and then, there are plenty of all of these, besides grasses of giant size, and splendid, lithe beauty, growing, in places, into a genuine bamboo. The cactus takes the place of the grasses wherever a very rocky or sandy spot repels other vegetation. Harpy eagles, vultures, kites and hawks soar over the *campos*. Woe to the small owl, or parrot, or rock-pigeon, which attempts to cross the *open*, instead of skirting the wood! woe to the small monkey who exposes himself in the too eager search for mimosa-pods or palm grubs! Sharp eyes are sure to see him, and sharp talons to seize him, and he is borne off, in spite of fearful squeals and gibberings. The war of nature goes on briskly here, both in the animal and vegetable world.

In the *campos* and savannas are seen plenty of humming-birds, of course, Brazil being the real home of the *Trochilidæ*. And here, too, are butterflies, the largest and most beautiful in the world, with high, rapid flight, like birds, going straight to their destination, not feeding much near the ground, but sucking the flowers upon the higher trees. As we cross a *campo* we frequently come upon the holes of the armadillo, with heaps of fresh earth thrown up around them, like mole-earths on a large scale. A queer-looking mongrel dog belonging to my guide sniffs and yaps at the holes, and would dig in if we had time to wait. The armadillos, as well as agoutis and opossums, are plentiful, and are all sought for, in moderation, by the Brazilians and negroes, who roast them, or bake them encased in clay. The smaller monkeys and the huge water-rats, which are so common, are frequently cooked in the same way, and considered very good eating. Of these animals, the monkeys, which pilfer fruit, and the opossums, which kill chickens, are considered vermin, while the agoutis and water-rats may be considered as game. But the littoral Brazilian has a very hazy idea about game at the best. As we pass along we see more birds, not only the ever-present humming-bird, poised before a flower, or darting like a bullet across our path, but many others of such brilliant plumage as to confound, in that respect, all the rest of the world. The doves and pigeons, of themselves, are sufficiently numerous and various to occupy an ornithologist for months. We heard a bell-bird, too, not very common on this island. The creature made a noise almost as loud and disagreeable as the ordinary steam-whistle, but, although he was evidently on the edge of the *campo*, and quite close to us, we could not see him. My guide seemed rather cowed by the cry, and I confess it was startling enough, at first, to make one feel a little ' spooky.'

There are huge spiders on the border of the *campo*, with thick, far-spreading, glutinous nets, almost fit to hold a calf. These giants of the *Arachnidæ* prey upon great beetles and small birds, sucking their life-juices as our spiders suck flies, and leaving their dried wing-cases and shriveled skins and bones and feathers, of azure, garnet, emerald and jet, flashing in the sunshine, but apparently useless in warning off others.

Bees of many kinds are busy among the flowers; the result of their labors, for the most part, never to be enjoyed by man. Many of them, indeed, most of them, are stingless. None of them are very large, and some are not larger than our house-fly. They make many kinds of honey, too, which is stored in hollow trees, or in clefts of rocks, or even in the earth. Some of it is perfectly liquid, and contained in sacks of wax, some is in combs; some of it is very sweet, some bitter. Some is green, some amber, some brown, or nearly black. A book about the bees of Brazil, if any man could find out all about them, would be a very large volume indeed.

I have already remarked that we found the remains of gorgeous beetles in the spider-webs, but this is not the hour to see the insects themselves in motion. They come out at nightfall, and rival the humming-birds in colors, and almost exceed them in size. Indeed, from this part of the empire come the beautiful coleoptera which are made into flowers and sprays and other ornaments, so celebrated, and now so dear. From these southern provinces, too, come most of the pearly fishscales, shells and feathers, which are made into beautiful ornaments by the 'sisters' at Santos, Rio de Janeiro and Bahia, although much of the work is produced at Sta. Catherina. People often wonder how they can imitate, from these materials, many of our flowers, such as roses and pinks and hyacinths, but it must be remembered that in this favored clime many of the flowers of the temperate zone flourish. The air is salubrious, and man flourishes too, when he lives according to ordinary sanitary rules, don't get wet too often, and does not take too much *cachaça* (the juice of the cane).

Having attempted hastily to describe some of the things which strike a stranger pleasantly in this sequestered spot, it is only fair to speak of some of the reptiles which infest these lovely scenes and constitute the disagreeable part of the subject. Of alligators, boas and anacondas, St. Catherine can show but few specimens, and those small and puny of their kind. But there are jararacás,—snakes whose bite is nearly always fatal, and they are quite plentiful withal. The "cobra coral" is a beautiful little snake, quite like the finest Neapolitan bracelet in color. It is said by the natives that he seldom, when suddenly come upon in the bush, lying among the flowers, allows one time to admire him, but darts forward and inflicts upon the face and neck a little nip, after which 'the subsequent proceedings' interest his admirer no more. Then there is the 'cobra sipo,' a much larger snake, four or five feet long, and the exact color of the 'sipos,' or lianas, among which he twines. He is capable of finishing, in short order, any animal, large or small, which comes within his reach. Another ghastly creature is the 'cobra fria,' or cold snake, which 'chills man's heart with cold' when crawling over him, and, if he moves, bites him to 'mors frigida.' Beside these there appears, on rough hill-sides and sandy, washed places, the rattlesnake, which most of us are apt to think of as confined to our northern hemisphere. When it was put upon one of the early Revolutionary flags of New England, I have no doubt that the makers thereof thought they were employing a local reptile to represent an idea. Instead of that the *Crotali* are distributed quite profusely in the southern as well as the northern hemisphere.

The day being now more than half spent, we turned westward again toward a point on the sound, where a boat was to meet me at sunset. The low range was again surmounted and crossed, the path leading us to the slippery stepping-stones of mountain streams and rivulets every few minutes. These little water-courses are kept full by the numerous showers, and are, even the largest, entirely unbridged. If a heavy rain temporarily swells them, the Brazilian merely sits down and waits until the excess of water has run off, as it does very soon, and the stepping-stones appear again. Upon reaching lower ground we began to find cultivation once more, mostly in small patches. There was sugar-cane, tobacco and cotton; palma Christi, for lamp-oil,—although the olive is not unknown in Southern Brazil,—and large patches of beans and vetches. Oranges again in plenty, and guavas, various useful palms, and always mandioc. Under the wild plantain or some forest-tree grows the cacao,—' food for the gods.'

Soon we came to huts, and then to houses,—and not too soon, for the usual afternoon rain came on, and we were glad to be housed during the heavy downpour, watching, meanwhile, the primitive household operations. The houses were all of one-story, terraced into the hillside, built of stone, and plastered, with tile roofs, and the walls painted or washed in some gaudy color. Almost all had cooking-sheds outside, consisting of thatched roofs, raised upon posts; and smaller shelter of the same kind contained the huge water-jars and drip-stones, or filters, raised on heavy tripods. Lovely jessamines and other climbing plants of great fragrance ran over the terrénos, or terraces, in front of these dwellings, growing with such luxuriance as to require frequent cutting, with no sparing hand. The habits of the people are such that no scent of jasmine or orange-blossom would overcome the smell from the household offal, thrown below the terrace, were it not for the scouring effect of the frequent rains on the hill-sides and the untiring exertions of the cur dogs, and the buzzards, and of myriads of ants, which, between them, soon clear off everything, even to the bones. The people were civil,—as those of Portuguese stock are apt to be,—and offered us what they had in the way of refreshments with perfect hospitality, refusing direct payment therefor. After a repast of flat mandioc-cake, hot from the griddle, goat-milk cheese, oranges, and a little cachaça, native cigars were produced, of very fair-flavored tobacco. These cigars do not keep well, however, for a worm soon attacks them, boring them through and through.

A perfect picture was the negress, Léocadia (they all have very fine names,—my guide's name was Agesiläus), who, in answer to the shout of 'Traga lumé, Léocadia!' brought us in from the cooking-place a live coal, which she rolled leisurely from one horny palm to the other, finally depositing it in the bowl of a spoon, from which we lighted our cigars. The woman was tall and lithe, but muscular, her jet-black skin shining with health, her eyes like sloes set in yellowish-white satin, teeth like a shark, and every one showing as she grins with delight at receiving a few *vintems*. She wears a bright handkerchief, which entirely conceals her woolly head, and, for all other clothing, a snow-white chemise, worn well off one shoulder, as usual, and a short, striped skirt.

When the shower was over we thanked our hosts, and pushed on toward the bay. The whole landscape was dripping and steaming as the afternoon sun came out, and the heavy rain-clouds floated away seaward. Soon the slippery path leads us to a cluster of tiny huts, perched on rocks, which overhang the waters of the beautiful bay, with several islands dotting its surface. On the largest of these—Rat Island, of course, for there is always a *Rat* island in every harbor of Brazil—is a dilapidated but picturesque old Portuguese fort. This stronghold I found, on subsequently visiting it, to be garrisoned by a garrulous, grizzled old sergeant, with at least a dozen large woolly dogs, looking like a cross breed between Newfoundlands and poodles. They were more amphibious than any dogs I have ever seen, and with good reason, for the sergeant's rations of *carne secca* and mandioc and beans not being more than sufficient to support his own little, shrivelled corpus, his dogs would have had a poor lookout on their rock unless they had managed to forage for themselves. This they did by forming line in a little shoal bay and driving before them shoals of tiny fish, like sprats, causing them to leap in their fright upon the sandy beach. They also swam to the mainland, where they searched the rocky shore, and made havoc among the eggs and young of gulls, pelicans and cormorants, having many a fight, and suffering many wounds from the sharp bills of the mother-birds. Sometimes they caught land-crabs under the mangroves, or, taking to the woods, they dug out the agoutis from their holes, or cut off some of the litter of a wild sow, or *javali*.

The inhabitants of the little village of which I have spoken seemed to be mostly fishermen. Several canoes of most primitive build were moored in a little cove, and near them were some men pottering over a heap of small oysters from the southern reef. There was also a pile of the shells of *murex*, which apparently had some commercial value, although, either from my dullness in comprehending the patois or from ignorance in my interlocutors, I could not learn where they were sent to. I suppose they must be used for the dye which they contain, like their Tyrian congeners of old.

Upon seeing me standing above, one of the men

detached himself from the group upon the beach, and, hobbling up the rough path, to my great surprise addressed me in English.

He was of miserable appearance, as sallow and unkempt as any of his associates, but with light eyes and hair, the first contrasting most unpleasantly with his dark face, while the hair was burnt by the sun until it had the appearance of tow. His clothing was filthy and ragged in the extreme, being of the coarse cloth, of yellowish-gray, which is used in Brazil for the slaves. As he walked with difficulty, my attention was attracted to his bare feet and legs, one of which was almost of the size and shape of that of an elephant, with the skin almost as much thickened and carunculated. His hands were scaly, and his fingers crooked like the claws of some obscene bird,—while his ears, behind which he carried one or two corn-shuck cigars, were curiously corrugated and split. He was a hopeless subject of elephantiasis,—the 'mal de San Lazaro.'

Questioning this poor creature, I found that he was by birth an American. God save the mark! He said he was forty,—he looked sixty-five. As he talked there was a queer sort of self-assertion and jauntiness about him when he used his mother-tongue, which he did somewhat imperfectly, and an abject whine and grimace when he relapsed into the Portuguese patois, as he constantly did.

'Give me a few *vintems*, sir! For God's sake, senhor! I have a hard time here—muito malo, senhor—to get a living!'

As my boat had not yet arrived, I asked him where he lived, and offered to go in the direction of the hut toward which he pointed. His face clouded, but as I walked toward the place he was forced to follow, stumping along as if he had fifty pounds of lead round his ankle. The hut was situated among huge boulders, which formed a part of the walls. It was built of rough stone, partially plastered, and with a palm thatch. The floor was the ground, damp, and sunken in the middle, and there was no furniture except some raw hides stretched upon sticks, and a few coarse earthenware jars and platters upon a sort of dresser of earth. The place had no light except that from the open door, and the smell was indescribably musty and unwholesome. The noise of our entrance caused a movement and chatter among the bats which were hanging from the thatch, while a lean, scrawny pig, which was rooting about the floor, dashed out with a snort as our shadows darkened the entrance, nearly upsetting us. A glance within was sufficient, and, smelling smoke, I passed round the corner of the hut and came upon the 'family,' squatting about a fire built between some stones under a palm-thatched shed, and partaking of a frugal meal of *bacalhao* and boiled yams. Bacalhao is the coarsest kind of cod, or haddock, or stock-fish, salted, and is the refuse, so to speak, of all the salt-fish put up in northern countries for exportation, while yam is not a delicacy, but requires *dura ilia* to extract from the coarse fibre the nourishing starchy particles. These people have fish for the catching, and eat them when they can get nothing else, but they seem seldom to smoke or salt them.

The family we found at their meal consisted of a wife, half mulatto and half negro,—a Zambo,—and three nearly naked children, from three to nine years old, with light eyes and muddy complexion. They all ceased eating and gazed up stupidly in wonder at our appearance, while their lord and master hovered in our rear in evident shame at the appearance of his family. There was no doubt the poor fellow was tied by the foot in more senses than one.

The place held out no temptation to remain very long, and I must say that I regretted coming at all, and thereby spying out the abject wretchedness of my new acquaintance. As if conscious of the self-reproach I felt, he followed me back to the beach, begging more humbly and persistently than ever for salted meat, American tobacco, and, above all, for *vintems*, his aspirations not apparently rising higher than those very clumsy and filthy copper coins. He did not say so, but I knew that they would be devoted to the purchase of the potent and nasty native rum, cachaça. A great deal of the sugar-cane of Brazil goes into cachaça, while in Rio Janeiro and other large towns the white beet-root sugar, from Belgium and France, is imported to fill the coffee-cups of the cafés. As an inducement to me to be charitable, I suppose, the poor cripple told me his miserable story, and, like the wedding-guest, I could not choose but hear, for I expected the boat to come for me at any moment, and I must await it there. The sun went down, and night came on fast, as I sat on a rock, with the goat-suckers and bats whirring and chirping round us while the man talked.

He said he was born in Rochester, New York, and had gone to school, like most American boys, until he was sixteen, when he had run away from home and become a sailor on the Lakes. Thence he had drifted to

New York, and was enlisted by an agent for a New Bedford whaler. The vessel made a bad voyage, and the skipper determined not to return home, so, running the ship into St. Catherine (a favorite resort for whalers), he committed barratry, selling the vessel, stores, outfit, and all, and leaving the crew (who were shipped on a 'lay,' or shares of the catch) to shift for themselves. Some of them soon shifted themselves out of the world with cachaça and foul living, others went to Santos or to Rio, and thence to sea again, while our friend, who had not strength of mind to do either, met his fate in the shape of that horrid woman of mahogany color and with hair like the stuffing of an old mattress. To complete his misery he soon became the subject of his hopeless and horrible disease.

He said that he did a little work, when he was able, picking over coffee on the terrénos, fishing or catching prawns, and sometimes interpreting, or selling fruit to chance vessels. But it was evident that he would not be able to do even that much longer, and it was fearful to think of the poor creature, reduced by his infirmity to spending his entire time in and about that damp, fetid cabin, with such surroundings and companionship. In this condition he might live, or rather survive, for years.

It was evident that there was not much to be done for him. As the coxswain of the boat (which just then came for me) remarked, in pertinent slang, 'His goose was cooked!' and here was another American citizen who had lost the chance of being president.

A lovely day had been saddened by the meeting with this unfortunate, about as great a wreck, in spite of the moralists, as any great city's most degrading vices could produce.

"There!" said the irrepressible Gasket, "I knew the doctor would throw cold water upon us in some way, and here he has made us all feel miserable by his story about that poor devil of a 'beach-comber.' Toggle! can't you give us something amusing to cheer us up?"

This request caused a merry laugh throughout the company at table, for Mr. Toggle, the second lieutenant, was noted not only for solemnity, but for taciturnity. Habitually sparing in words, he was also never known to laugh, for, while all the necessary motions of the facial muscles took place when a good joke was produced, no sound of cachinnation was ever heard to issue from his throat. Use had accustomed his messmates to this peculiarity, and he was held in high estimation by those inclined to talk. After remarking that he "was a poor hand at a yarn," which no one present attempted in the least to controvert, every one expected him to relapse into silence; but, to the astonishment of his hearers, this last Christmas dinner seemed to have "greased his talking tacks," and he went on to say that he would try to give them some reminiscences of a Christmas he spent in Panama under rather peculiar circumstances, when the temperature and surroundings were little in keeping with the usual ideas concerning the festive season.

"In 18——," said Mr. Toggle, "the quaint old city was occupied by a force from our ships. We had landed quite a large body of men, whose presence prevented the revolutionists, in the 'pronunciamento' then in action, from plundering or molesting the foreign population, or from damaging native property to any great extent. This we effected without any actual collision with the revolutionists; and some of the older men, who had been in the war, seemed to think the expedition a very tame one, because there was no shooting. But we had several alarms and a few funny scenes.

One very dark night I was sleeping in a hammock swung between two of the pillars of the old cabildo, facing the plaza, when I was awakened by a sentry's hail, followed by excited whispering quite near me, and strange, unearthly noises in the distance across the square. Of course I was up in an instant, and saw the guard turn out, with a couple of lanterns which feebly lit the scene for a few yards around. The sentry who had hailed was posted over the artillery parked in front of the main entrance of the cabildo. He was a Welsh forecastle-man, nicknamed 'Taffy' by the men, and his next man was an afterguardsman, named O'Brien, a Milesian, *pur sang*, who was on post No. 1, in front of the main guard.

From their hurried conversation with each other I gathered that they had both heard some movement on the other side of the plaza, upon which they had hailed and received so unintelligible and unusual a reply that they were about to fire on the intruders. As we were in a delicate position, and acting rather as a police force than as an army of occupation, they were promptly ordered to hold their fire, but to continue on the alert. The disturbing element continued to advance and retreat, never answering, except by incoherent noises, and keeping all hands upon the *qui vive*, yet never coming so near the danger-line as to necessitate a shot. Finally, the break of day revealed a grazing donkey, indulging occasionally in the varied notes for which a Panama 'burro' is so celebrated, and I heard the artillery sentry call out to post No. 1, ' Never mind the guard ; it's only an Irish butterfly!'

Paddy, who had made out the enemy by this time, retorted, 'Bedad! Taffy, me boy, you're mistaken! for by the length of his ears I know him to be a Welsh rarebit!'

We had orders, continued Lieutenant Toggle, not to allow troops, arms, or ammunition to pass over the Panama Railroad; and if any of the latter did come, not to deliver them until the troubles were over.

Miller, our master-at-arms, was acting as sergeant-major of the force, and had been detailed to inspect all freight which might arrive at the depot. One day he came to me in a very mysterious and solemn way and requested my presence at the freight-house. On the way he told me that ten barrels of flour had arrived by train, addressed to a negro who kept a small corner-grocery just outside our lines, whom we knew to be one of the principal purveyors to the revolutionists.

The anxiety shown by this man to get his flour, as well as the unusual weight of the barrels, had aroused Miller's suspicions, and he now wanted my sanction and presence at a closer inspection. Upon reaching the freight-room the doors were closed, the head of one of the barrels immediately knocked in, and a few prods with a ramrod revealed some hard substance beneath the flour, the removal of which discovered a gunny-bag full of fixed ammunition. An examination of the other nine barrels gave the same result. There were ten thousand cartridges in all,—quite enough to have kept the revolution going for at least a week.

My first impulse was to seize the consignment, flour and all, as contraband, but Miller finally induced me to deliver the flour, which was certainly harmless, acknowledging that he had a plan by which he could get square with the consignee, against whom our men bore a heavy grudge for having swindled them in the sale of some cheese. Miller was well known among our crew as a wag, and I withdrew to wait for the fun which I made sure would follow.

The ship's cooper and two or three men were sent for, and in a short time the cartridges were replaced by old railroad spikes, the barrels headed up neatly, and the traces of flour carefully swept up from the floor. Miller then sent for Pancho, the grocery-keeper, who had been anxiously waiting outside the lines with a dozen men and a large dray, and told him he could remove his flour, but must not bring his dray any nearer, as it was against orders to have any drays cross the plaza.

Our men had had a hint of the proceedings from Miller, and all who were not on post turned out to see the 'Greasers' tugging and perspiring in the scorching Panama sun as they painfully lugged the heavy barrels one by one clear across the plaza. The dray was finally loaded, and Pancho, grinning at the way in which he had 'done' the Yankees, mounted on the top of his treasure and started for his shop, drawn by his baker's dozen of ragged rascals. The 'bodega' was surrounded by a crowd of the 'revolutionists,' as eager for cartridges as the boys of a New England village are for fire-crackers on the third of July. The barrels were rolled in amidst shouts of joy and jeers of derision at the gullibility of the 'Gringos;' but the triumph was not of long duration, and the peals of scornful laughter soon gave way to yells of anger and a perfect Pandemonium of gestures and curses, such as could only be gotten up with success in this one locality.

Pancho himself soon appeared, foaming with rage and making the air blue with curses. He started straight for our lines, apparently with the intention of demanding redress, but he was promptly halted by the sentinels, and received with such jeers and volleys of laughter by our men that, after glaring round him, stamping, and tearing his hair for some minutes, he beat a final retreat,—a poorer, if not a wiser man."

"Well done, Toggle," said Gasket, by this time quite beyond the ordinary amenities. "I always thought you *could* talk, if you only tried."

"Ah, Gasket," replied Toggle, mildly shaking his head, "it isn't always those who talk most who have most to say."

Gasket evidently thought that something was implied by this remark; but, before he could bring his mind thoroughly to bear upon it, the flag-officer (who had not forgotten his mess-table experiences) said, in rather more of an official tone than he was wont to assume on such occasions,—

"If Mr. Gasket has no story to give us, I, for one, shall be glad to hear from Mr. Inkham."

The slight cloud which had come over the harmony of the evening instantly cleared away, and all eyes were turned upon the admiral's secretary.

The secretary was a character rather well known throughout the whole service.

A friend, or professing friend, of every one, he was, nevertheless, usually reserved in manner, and diplomatic and oracular to a degree.

He never took less than an hour for the composition of any official paper whatever; after which the fair copying had to be effected by the clerk, even if it was so simple a document as thanks for a salute, or congratulations upon the birth of a princess.

The drawing up of "charges and specifications of charges," in the matter of a general court-martial, or some such weighty business, was a case in which he felt constrained to retire for a time altogether from public view, keeping within his own den, or office, on the gun-deck. Here he had beef-tea and strong coffee sent him at intervals, while he kept his head wrapped in a wet towel—and thought. After this fortification and preparation he was accustomed to consult the "Revised Statutes" and "Harwood's Procedure."

That kind of thing would be kept up for an unlimited period, according to the disposition of the flag-officer with whom he was serving. When the admiral could not be kept quiet any longer, and began to show decided impatience and annoyance at his secretary's delay, the document was produced, not in sheets, but in fragmentary notes; some such scraps as Shelley or Byron might have written, in their inspired moments, on the first paper at hand.

The "writer" then went to work to reduce these to order, while the secretary emerged upon the gun-deck, —somewhat disheveled as to his scanty locks,—and, for hours, puffed volumes of cigar smoke, while, with bared brow, he rested his brain from its labors.

These mental struggles had been going on for a good many years, and the secretary was, to speak within bounds, not any longer a young man.

Hirsute as to lip and chin, the dome which had so long contained this pregnant brain was polished like ivory, and had wisps of rusty gray hair brought up from the back and meandering over the top in an artificial manner,—as "Jack" puts it, "the after-guard were obliged to do foretopmen's duty."

With all these little peculiarities (barring occasional petulance, the usual accompaniment of genius), Inkham was not at all a bad messmate, and had so succeeded in making friends throughout the service that his old companions, as they rose to command, always felt themselves obliged to do something for "Old Ink," and many thought themselves lucky if they could secure his valuable services for a cruise.

He was really much more naval in his ideas (except where discipline conflicted with his personal comfort), and more military in bearing and beard, and a greater stickler for forms, than if he had borne a commission.

His father, a commander in the navy, had died on board one of the old " Commissioner's sloops" (the only command he ever had), being then about fifty-eight.

He had taken to sea with him his son, aged eighteen, as his clerk, "with a view to his health and general education."

The son's health improved,—to the extent that ship's whisky would allow,—and his education (especially in billiards) was so thoroughly finished that Inkham remained a captain's clerk for many cruises.

When time, in its benign way, had silvered his hair and beard, and given him an appearance of dignity and wisdom, he "bore up" for a secretaryship, and had been a secretary ever since.

Inkham was an admirer of Byron, and often wrote verses himself, and his knowledge of naval events and of naval men, *of his own time*, was marvelous, and extended back to the war with Mexico.

His knowledge of novels and periodical literature was also immense, but he remembered nothing whatever of history, naval or other, in which he had not himself borne a part; and had always to post up on that kind of thing for the occasion.

Sometimes he talked of Vattel, Puffendorf, Wheaton and Phillimore; really knowing nothing about these authorities. But, by these references, wise looks, and the possession of a certain diplomatic slang, he imposed upon youngsters, who considered that they were improving their minds if they could detain him half an hour longer than usual on the gun-deck, by the judicious administration of their choicest cigars and most delicate flattery.

He was also supposed by these young gentlemen to be the repository of the flag-officer's secrets, and to know, even if he did not inspire, the whole operations of the squadron months in advance; which was more than anyone else knew, however high in authority.

After he withdrew from these nightly tobacco parliaments, his admirers would wag their heads, and say to each other, "Devilish deep fellow, Old Inkham. Pity he was choused out of that consul-generalship at Milo."

If he had remembered all he had seen and read Inkham *would* have been a " devilish deep fellow." In fact, if he had profited by his numberless acquaintances and extended experience, he should have brought up in some safe haven of rest and plenty long before.

But his life had been perfectly objectless and futile, wasted on petty intrigues for " the next cruise," which was to bring him nothing, and to leave him in the same position,—only so many years older.

He always spent every penny of his pay on his back and stomach, and never saved a dollar; but then, to do him justice, he always looked and lived like a gentleman.

Inkham had two maiden sisters, of about his own age, who believed in him, and who received him, whenever he came back from his sea-rovings (much more willingly as he grew older and ceased his wiles), into the mansion where they maintained a select school for young ladies. Here he remained, eating the fatted calf, and fluttering the hearts of those doves, until he got another appointment.

As time went on he found out that the girls (many generations of whom had passed under his critical eye) had come to call him "Old Ink," and then he cut his sisters, and, when on shore, established himself in grimy lodgings, and lived at a second-rate club.

Of the luxurious furniture and general gorgeousness of this club he was wont to give glowing descriptions to the junior officers with whom he sailed, thereby beguiling many a long evening on a tedious passage.

With all this, as we have said, " Ink " wasn't half a bad fellow.

Was a midshipman suffering from fever, no one was more ready than " Ink" to volunteer for a night's watch, and no one was more willing to sit and read for hours to a sufferer with a broken leg or inflamed eyes, while he vied with the chaplain in writing letters and transacting business for "Jack," if the latter only approached him in the right way.

The secretary, on being called upon by his immediate chief, at once responded, and said:

"I have one Christmas recollection which will remain with me forever, and I will try to give you the event as it occurred.

In the month of December, 1863, I was captain's clerk in the old *Blazer*, at New Orleans. Important dispatches were to go North, and, as our way through Dixie was then obstructed, I was selected to carry them by sea.

In twenty-four hours after receiving the orders I had packed up, bid good-by to my comrades of Farragut's squadron, packed my dispatches in a water-proof bag, and was under way for New York, a passenger in the *Mariposa*, a propeller of about fifteen hundred tons, built for the New Orleans and Galveston trade just before the war, and then running irregularly between the Crescent City and New York, sometimes calling at Havana.

Before the *Mariposa* reached the quarantine ground, I had made the acquaintance of her skipper, Captain Waverly, a handsome, dapper little fellow, of about thirty, very precise in manner, and dandified in costume; something of a ladies' man, too, if one might judge from the gallant manner in which he pointed out the historical places on either bank of the river to our two lady passengers,—daughters of a New York banker, who was also on board.

The mate seemed to be in charge of the ship, and impressed me as being a fair specimen of the merchant seaman, and evidently something of a tartar, from his arbitrary manner and rather profane language when addressing his crew, a nondescript set, made up, to all appearance, about equally of wharf-rats from New York and steamboat-hands picked up at New Orleans.

The second mate was a mild-mannered youth, whose stupidity in fishing the anchor soon brought him in for a good sound cursing from the lips of the chief officer.

The latter bustled about in a lively way, completing the stowage of the cargo, securing the boats and loose articles about the decks, and finally, when the pilot left us, at the mouth of the river, setting the course and taking the departure; the captain not appearing to interest himself in anything but the comfort of the ladies.

We had left New Orleans before daylight, and night had fallen when we stood out into the Mexican Gulf, soon after which time we were called to a late dinner, when I made the acquaintance of my fellow-passengers. These were few, and consisted of the New York financier and his two daughters (I strongly suspected that the old gentleman was not remotely connected with the cotton speculations then going on); a young and interesting-looking colonel of Massachusetts Volunteers, who was going home on sick-leave; a bright young fellow who had been sent down on some business for a New York mercantile house, and a grave, reserved, and rather sad-looking man of about thirty, who was introduced as Mr. Jones, and who appeared to have no particular calling.

The dapper captain had the banker on his right, and the eldest and prettiest daughter on his left, at the table, and he seemed disposed to monopolize the conversation of the latter, in spite of the endeavors of the young commercial traveler to enter the lists against him.

When I went on deck to smoke my after-dinner cigar I found the first mate on watch, and, as he spoke to me politely and seemed inclined to talk, I joined him in his walk.

After a few trivial remarks about the fineness of the night, I soon found myself listening to a very fervent growl at the stupidity of " the owners " in putting such a vessel as the *Mariposa* in charge of such a captain. The mate went on to inform me that Captain Waverly was the nephew of one of the owners, was a good theoretical navigator, but had been fifteen years at sea without becoming a seaman, and was a good deal fonder of the ladies than he was of his business.

Nothing more was needed to convince one of the inefficiency of the skipper than that his chief officer dared to talk in this way to a passenger.

Of course I did not relish this kind of harangue, and looked to see if the man was drunk, but he was not, and I soon threw away my cigar, bade the old 'shell-back' good-night, and went below to turn in, my conscience rather reproaching me for listening so long to abuse of the captain from the lips of his subordinate.

It is just possible that this quickening was hastened by Captain Waverly's sending me a nice glass of grog, with his compliments and best wishes for a good night's rest. It was evident that he knew how to do the honors of his ship, at any rate.

The next day, and the two succeeding ones, passed without incidents of an unusual kind.

The *Mariposa* was a fast ship, and we had had a fair wind and an unusually smooth sea, in consequence of which we were making an excellent run, and fully expected to round Cape Hatteras the following night, and, as it was now the 23d of the month, to be at home, in New York, on Christmas-day.

I had not spent a Christmas at home for several years, and was anxious to drop in on some relations on that day, knowing well how cordially I would be received.

Sitting and smoking on deck, and filled with these thoughts of home and friends, and of the happy Christmas times passed in my boyhood, I was rather startled by the abrupt approach of the captain, who broke in upon my reverie by saying, ' Well, Mr. Inkham, we are not to escape without a taste of bad weather, after all. I think, from the movements of the barometer, that a northeaster is likely to catch us off Hatteras, and, unless all signs fail, we shall have a good stiff blow to-night. However, it is just possible that we may make Hampton Roads before the gale strikes us.'

I replied to the captain that both he and myself were somewhat used to rough weather, but that pretty Miss Nellie Banker would probably be dreadfully frightened.

'It's an ill wind which blows nobody good, captain. Who knows but this may give you a chance to distinguish yourself, and may blow you a rich and pretty wife?'

The skipper smiled broadly at the idea, and went across the deck to hold a consultation with his first officer, who was leaning on the weather-rail and casting dubious glances, first at the sky and then at the skipper, and, every now and then, looking over at me and shaking his head, as much as to say, 'There'll be the devil to pay soon, and no pitch hot.'

Not feeling any responsibility in regard to the navigation of the ship, I had not observed the weather very closely. Now, however, my attention was aroused, and, on looking at the horizon, I saw in the northeast an inky-black cloud, which looked darker than any squall I had ever seen before.

Walking to the companion-way, I found to my horror that the barometer which hung there stood at the unusually low point of twenty-eight degrees. The sea was at this time almost perfectly smooth, and the light breeze which had been blowing during the afternoon had died out, so that the smoke from our chimney was trending right aft.

Whilst I was making these observations I was joined by Mr. Jones, who remarked that 'if he were at home in Delaware County, he should say we were going to have some rain.'

A few minutes afterward Captain Waverly came on deck, and, after taking a look at the sky, turned to the chief mate and said, 'That cloud looks as if it might give us a wetting, and it may be followed by a little wind. If it comes out fair, get the topsails and fore and aft sails on her.'

The mate, with a curious expression of doubt clearly depicted on his weather-beaten countenance, suggested that, instead of making a lot of sail, it would be better at once to get the close reef in the main-topsail and stand by for a 'lay-to.'

THE SECRETARY'S STORY.

This the skipper would not listen to, but in a very peremptory manner directed the mate to carry out his orders; then, turning, he started to go down the companion-way.

By this time I had become thoroughly interested in the way things were going, and I was not surprised to see the captain's face turn white as he glanced at the barometer. He at once hurried back to the bridge, and the hands were instantly called to put a close reef in the main-topsail and to bend the fore storm-staysail and storm-mizzen.

In an instant there was great excitement and some confusion. Even the passengers were sufficiently aroused by this time to lend a hand, and I found myself first tugging aft on the storm-mizzen and then doing my best to assist in bending it. At my side I recognized Jones, who, to my surprise, seemed to be perfectly at home in the operation, and, instead of being only an assistant, soon took charge of the whole business. The unusual noise and bustle soon brought on deck the ladies, who had, with their father and the colonel, been having a game of whist.

So busy was I at my work that I had not again looked at the weather, and was therefore taken rather aback when a tremendous squall, which struck us all at once, caused every timber in the ship to creak, and spar to buckle.

The ship went over almost on her beam-ends, and had it not been for the hatch-coamings, houses, and high net-work railings, most of us aft would have been spilled into the sea.

I heard the engine-room gong strike 'four bells,' and

the rudder-chains rattle and clank as the helm was put hard up. Then the men scrambled forward to the storm-staysail halliards.

To my joy I saw that she paid off and was soon running before the wind, which had come out with fearful force from the northeast.

The sun had gone down by this time and we were soon in pitchy darkness. The main-topsail, which had been loosed, and partly reefed, ballooned, and with the wind which filled it caused the ship to bury forward and to yaw frightfully.

Fortunately, the sea was still quite smooth.

The mate and the captain were together on the bridge, but I could plainly make out, by his frenzied gestures, that the latter had quite lost his head, and that the little which was being done originated with the chief officer.

Jones and I managed to work our way to the after-compass, and a look at that revealed the skipper's intentions.

'My God!' said Jones, as soon as he had a glimpse of the card, 'the man is crazy! He is setting a course for the capes, directly across the track of a veritable hurricane, blowing him right on the land, to say nothing of the strong current which will soon be trending in the same direction. A very few hours of this work will finish us.'

With this remark I noticed an entire change in Jones's manner. His lips were compressed, his hands clinched harder than ever the rope to which we were clinging, and he was evidently laboring to control some strong impulse.

The sea had, by this time, begun to run very high,

and once or twice green water had come over our quarter. The ship was yawing fearfully, and more than once almost fell off into the trough of the sea. We had already succeeded in closing and battening all the hatches and companions aft, seeing every one in the cabin on deck, and lashing the banker and his daughters to one of the standing settees on the cabin hatch. The colonel, Jones and myself had secured ourselves just forward of the after wheel-house, and there waited events.

Suddenly, Jones turned to the colonel and myself, and said, 'You are both in the government service, and presumably brave men. Will you back me if I take command of this ship and try to save her?'

I had been impressed with Jones's behavior since the beginning of the storm, and had become convinced that he was a seaman in disguise.

The colonel must have come to about the same conclusion. At any rate, we both promised, at once, not only to back him with moral support, but to lend him our personal assistance.

Jones, after a look of unmistakable tenderness toward the ladies lashed on the hatch, cast himself adrift, and started slowly to make his way to the bridge, followed by the colonel and myself. Reaching the bridge-ladder, he turned to us and said, 'I am going on the bridge to take charge. The captain is thoroughly incapacitated through ignorance and fear, and the mate is a sailorman, but nothing more, and will probably be glad to have some one assume responsibility. You two must get some of the hands together and induce them to go aloft and cut away that maintopsail. Then I shall attempt to bring the ship to; and you must get a corner of the storm-mizzen on her.'

With this Jones went up on the bridge, and returned in a moment, followed by the mate, who thoroughly understood the situation, if he could not master it.

Jones simply told us to carry out his orders; but, after some time spent in a search for the men, we returned to our new captain with only two seamen, whom we had found under the break of the forecastle. The rest had not been used to such emergencies, and had stowed themselves below, securely, in the many places afforded by a vessel built like the *Mariposa*. These two seamen, when we got them aft, said it was blowing too hard for them to go aloft, and that the sail had better blow away. But it might not blow away soon enough, and its effect was very bad in the mean time.

Although I was no sailor, I had been a long time with sailors, and knew about what was to be done; so, turning to Jones, I said, 'I will go on one yard-arm.' The mate at once offered to try the other. Borrowing a knife from one of the recreant seamen, I put it between my teeth and started to get into the rigging.

Although the wind was fearful in strength to those upon deck, it was nothing to the blast as I attempted to go aloft. My feet were at times blown from under me, and I was straightened out like a pennant; at other times I was pinned flat against the shrouds for minutes; and it was only with the utmost exertion, and at the cost of considerable bodily pain and suffering, that I succeeded, in the course of half an hour, in reaching the horns of the trestle-trees. After ten minutes more of hard and exhausting work I reached the yard, and found that the mate was already slashing away on the weather yard-arm, cutting the robands from the slings out.

I started to do the same on the lee yard-arm, and was working away with a will, and holding on like grim death as I swayed above the hell of waters below, when, with a report like a cannon, the whole sail was suddenly torn from the yard and disappeared in the inky blackness to leeward.

Our task was accomplished, and, after long and severe exhaustion, I succeeded in reaching the deck, utterly exhausted.

I found that Jones and the colonel, assisted by the two seamen and the quartermasters, who remained at the wheel, had attempted to heave the ship to, without success. They had also tried to set the storm-mizzen, but had been unsuccessful, as that sail had followed the topsail and fore storm-staysail, all of which had gone to leeward during my absence aloft.

The after wheel-house had been washed away, as well as the small saloon over the cabins. The boats were all gone, and every movable object, as well as many supposed to be immovable, had followed them. Fortunately, the after skylight, with its precious freight, was well secured and remained in place.

Captain Waverly now came aft from the bridge, and, seeming to regain some little confidence, offered to assist us.

Jones decided to make another effort to bring the ship to. His idea was, on putting the helm down, to spread something about the mizzen rigging to throw her head up, and so assist the engine and the helm in bringing her by the wind.

I was so bruised and exhausted that I felt that, even to save my life, I could do but little more.

The colonel now came to the front, and offered to try to spread a tarpaulin, which we found becketed to the skylight, in the mizzen rigging, and Captain Waverly and the mate offered to assist him.

When all was ready, Jones started for the bridge again, and we soon found the ship's motion changing, and that the new captain was endeavoring to put her round. I got back to my position by the mizzen rigging, where the mate and the colonel had the tarpaulin so made up that the wind itself would assist in unrolling it if they could only succeed in getting it into proper position in the shrouds.

Their first attempt was to get up inboard, and was perfectly fruitless. They then attempted to get outboard, but the ship had come-to so much by this time that she was in the trough of the most infernal sea I had ever seen. Our rolling was something fearful. The yard-arms dipped, and green seas were carried whole from one bulwark to the other, and had anything been left about the deck it must have surely gone.

One roll soon came worse than all the rest, so deep that it seemed hardly possible that we ever could right again. In fact, it was too much for the masts, all three of which snapped off like pipe-stems, and were soon wallowing and thumping along our side, to its immediate danger.

Their fall, however, relieved us considerably, and we redoubled our efforts in consequence.

The mate succeeded in getting hold of the pole of the mizzen-topmast, which had been broken off, and to this we lashed the tarpaulin with a piece of the signal halliards, making a yard of it. This yard, we with infinite trouble, placed up and down the stump of the mizzenmast and lashed it there by the middle, and, having bent on braces to its ends, suddenly swayed it across to windward. Our sail filled against the stump, and to our great joy, did not blow away.

By this time daylight was with us again, and Jones, on the bridge, was enabled to witness our success.

Fortunately, during all these long hours the engine and boilers had worked well. Owing to the care and ingenuity of the chief engineer, and to the pluck with which his department had stuck to their work during that terrible night, no water had come into the engine-room, and the hull of the ship had remained tight.

An extra jump of the engines, aided by our sail, and a judicious use of the helm at a comparatively smooth moment, brought us by the wind.

Jones now ordered us to rig a similar sail on the stump of the foremast, which we succeeded in doing in much shorter time, owing to having daylight, and we were now hove to and comparatively safe, although the sea was more fearful to look at than ever.

The hurricane (for it had the force of one, although it did not shift) continued until about an hour before sunset, when it suddenly lulled, and as suddenly chopped round to the northwest, blowing again with fearful violence.

During the lull we managed to get some hard bread and water from the forecastle, as well as some tarpaulin coats for the ladies, who were shivering in the blast in their drenched garments.

We shifted our storm-sails, and, being able to do no

more, secured ourselves, and hoped for the best. The effect of the shift of wind was soon apparent. The motion had been bad enough before, but it had now become indescribable, as a cross-sea of tremendous violence arose. We pitched and rolled, turned and twisted, while every timber, bolt, and knee, from stem to stern, and from the keel to our mast-stumps, groaned and complained in a most ominous manner. Worse than all, the ship now began to make water rapidly, numerous leaks occurring from the wrenching she received; and soon after the engines stopped. There seemed now to be no hope for us; but a look at our poor, half-dead lady passengers gave us new strength, and, hauling out the recreant steamboat-hands from their hiding-places, we rigged the deck-pumps, and went to work at them with a will.

As if to encourage us, the wind now shifted to the westward, and soon subsided to a gentle breeze, while the cross-seas seemed to kill each other, and at two A.M. we were lying, a water-logged hulk, on a comparatively smooth sea.

A few hours after, by great good fortune, a large navy tug (which had come out of Beaufort after the gale) sighted us, bore down, and took us in tow.

The men now turned to, and managed to keep the water under; and, as we had valuable government stores as cargo, the skipper of the tug considered himself justified in taking us into Hampton Roads. The ship was safely brought in, and in twenty-four hours afterwards the passengers were all in New York.

It so happened that, on the 24th of December, 1864, the vessel to which I was then attached arrived at the Brooklyn Navy-Yard.

When the mail came on board I found an invitation to the wedding of Lieutenant Johns, of the navy, and Miss Banker, accompanied by a very flattering note from the lady, urging my acceptance of the invitation.

It is hardly necessary to say that I was not only at the church, but afterwards attended the reception, which took place in a stately mansion, filled with flowers, light, and the strains of charming music, while gay crowds of lovely women and comely men congratulated the newly-married pair.

The contrast between this scene and that awful Christmas-eve off Hatteras, only one year before, was a very marked one, and yet several of the persons present had filled a place upon both occasions.

I am sure that not one of the guests wished more heartily than I did that the gallant groom might find life's voyage, in matrimonial seas, a pleasant one."

When the secretary had finished his story it was evident that the usually imperturbable first lieutenant was blushing furiously, and, although no explanations were given, it was not difficult to draw a conclusion as to who was the hero of the story.

"I notice," said the first lieutenant, "that we have heard nothing whatever from the senior marine officer this evening, and as few people in the mess have a more varied acquaintance and experience, I feel sure he will oblige us with a reminiscence."

"Yes, Ratchet," said the caterer, "do give us something. There is surely time enough left for that." And he glanced inquiringly at Captain Tangent, who was evidently revolving in his mind the propriety of a move.

The captain of marines was not a tall man,—in point

of fact he was rather a short man,—but he looked tall, because he stood so very straight that he almost bent backward.

His orderly sergeant, who was six feet two, looked positively abject and diminutive beside his officer when he brought his morning report to be signed, and heard, with soldierly patience and at strict "attention," the harangue which Captain Ratchet delivered upon the shameful state of Private Jenkin's pantaloons at evening quarters on the day before.

Captain Ratchet had moustaches and imperial, waxed after the manner of the late lamented Napoleon III., and was upon all occasions as neat in dress as it is possible for mortal man to be.

His most intimate friend could never find out how many shirts and neckties and pairs of white gloves the captain possessed. Perhaps he did not know himself. At any rate, the supply was practically inexhaustible.

His state-room was a model bower, full of photographs, *curios*, and neat little "kickshaws," and contained, beside, two shelves which held his "library," which consisted of the Bible, Hardee's Tactics, the "School of the Soldier," an elementary treatise on fortification and defense, and two or three odd volumes of the *Gentleman's Magazine*, with the name, arms, and motto of his grand-uncle, John, of Greencastle, emblazoned on the covers.

Under these, on a rack, hung his ivory-handled Mameluke sword, with the white belt swathed around it; a small silk guidon which he himself had taken in battle; his favorite Powhatan pipe, with reed stem; and a tobacco-bag, embroidered by fair hands, with the captain's monogram in red silk.

Back of his berth he had piles of French novels and of the *Spirit of the Turf and Field*, a gentleman's newspaper,—for the captain was a great authority upon all "events" in either hemisphere.

He knew the precise number of rounds in which the "Hoboken Pet" had licked the "Bowery Buster;" the figures earned at the first and second innings by the Stenton Cricket Club when playing the Aberdeen professionals; how many pigeons Dr. Cutler had to spare when he beat Captain Bogler; and the exact time of all the trotters from Lady Suffolk to Maud S.

Captain Ratchet was also an inexhaustible talker upon political subjects, and he had rather a propensity to bet upon elections.

Besides doing all these things, the captain sang and played on the guitar, and, since he made an European cruise, indulged principally in French military *chansonnettes*, such as

> "Ran tan plan, c'est la cantinière,
> Un joli soldat!
> Ran tan plan, qui va la première
> Quand la tambour bat."

or,

> "Quand l'zouzou, coiffé de son fez,
> A par hasard, queuqu' goutt' sous l'nez.

His messmates got to know some of these songs pretty well, but then that is not surprising in a three years' cruise.

With all these little weaknesses (and which one of us, let me ask, had fewer?), the captain was truthful, temperate, a good son and brother, and the cheeriest and most obliging of messmates.

He held a brevet for gallant service in the army, where bullets were flying thickly, and death or wounds from them were meeting every second man, and, to tell the truth, when many of those about him were not preserving that coolness, readiness, and serene courage which rendered little Ratchet one of the heroes of the day.

Ratchet had entered the marine corps from the volunteer service, and had already seen his share of hard fighting when he received his commission; while every one who knew him knew also that, at any hour of the day or night, at sea or on shore, he stood ready to see hard fighting again, and to attend to the details thereof with the same thoroughness and deliberation with which he was wont to inspect the "kit" of his guard on Friday morning.

In fact and altogether, Ratchet was one of the kind of people who "wear well," and although his messmates might occasionally smile at some little foible or peculiarity, there were none of them who did not sincerely wish him all good, and feel that they could rely upon him in an emergency.

Though uniformly patient and good-natured during the trials and annoyances of a cruise, Ratchet at heart hated every other place in the world but Washington.

" Talk to him of the band of the Twenty-first Austrian Infantry! Had they ever heard the Marine Band at Washington? Fifty-pieces, sir!"

"Talk about the Tuileries!" the captain would say. "Have you seen the new department buildings at Washington, sir?"

In his rare naps Ratchet dreamed of passing the autumn of his life at the Washington barracks, and of attending endless levées and receptions, while, at the head of a thoroughly well-uniformed and well-drilled battalion of marines, he escorted successive Presidents to their inauguration. Or, should death perchance have chosen a shining mark, he equally (and equably, in his dreams) escorted the remains to their destination.

Without more ado, and taking a preliminary sip of claret, his favorite wine, the captain proceeded as follows:

"Well, to begin with, I'm no hand at this sort of thing. Story-telling is not my forte; and if it were, it would long ago have become a lost art for want of practice. You all know very well that, for a modest man like myself, it is impossible to get in a word edgewise in this wardroom.

Another thing, the yarn I'm going to tell you doesn't redound to the credit of the naval reputation for acuteness very hugely. On the contrary it shows that however much some men may circumnavigate the world, they really know precious little of it. You'll all call me a vilifier, no doubt, for the authorities quotable scout all idea of a landsman outwitting a sailor,—Marryatt and Cooper, Gringo, in his 'Tales for the Marines,' Davy Llewellyn, in 'The Maid of Sker,' will tell you no end of instances where Jack Tar overreaches the lobsters to one where any man, from lord high sheriff to bumboatman, can outwit him. It's only when the other sex takes hold that you capitulate.

But you were sold this time, and no mistake. It was away back in '66, so soon after the war that uniforms were still familiar sights all over the Northern towns and cities; even on Fifth Avenue and Broadway a fellow could appear in the garb of his profession without being treated with indignity; and in the bright September of that year it was my luck to be, for a few days, in the harbor of New London. Two or three of our ships had been there off and on, and just at this time one of our best, with as smart a set of officers, in their own opinion, as is often found even in our navy, was lying off Fort Trumbull. Two batteries of the First Artillery were stationed in the old fort at the time, and among their officers was a particular friend of mine, a first lieutenant and a West-Pointer, a graduate of the class of '63, and I'll call him Ford.

Ferguson, over there is beginning to look conscious and uneasy already. Never mind, old fellow, I'll name no names, even of the ships; but you remember, don't you, the day a whole batch of you juniors went over to call upon the officers of the *Themis*, the flag-ship of the French squadron? I see you do, so we'll go ahead.

It seems that while aboard the flag-ship, and having a most enjoyable, not to say convivial, time with the Frenchmen, there came into their midst a party of people from shore, young gentlemen of the vicinity, apparently, who were desirous of seeing the ship, but, being unacquainted with the French language or the French officers, might have been at a loss how to proceed but for the self-possession and *savoir faire* of a handsome little fellow in a jaunty artillery uniform, who promptly introduced himself as Captain Dyer, of the regular army, was greeted with the utmost civility by the officers of the ship, was by them presented to our fellows there present; and, in a few minutes, the entire party was on terms of delightful companionship, the young New-Englander showing

THE MARINE OFFICER'S STORY. 167

as keen an appreciation of the bountiful supplies of Bordeaux, Sauterne, or Cognac as though they never expected to see the outside of the "land of steady habits." But the central figure, the hero of the occasion, to judge from the talk of Ferguson and his friends when they returned to us that evening—— Oh! beg pardon, Ferguson. I *did* say I'd mention no names, but you see Mark Twain is responsible for the slip. Ever since the birth of the 'Innocents Abroad' your name has become the universal symbol of an unknown person, as X is of an unknown quantity. The central figure, as I was saying, was that of young Captain Dyer. He could not speak French, but he was so full of life, enthusiasm, and —well, they *did* say—cheek, that he kept the ball of conversation rolling, and the Frenchmen hung around him with absolute fascination. He had astonished them, on his first appearance, it seemed, by the extreme juvenility of his face and figure, and, seeing this, he had modestly hastened to explain, 'I'm not a full captain of artillery, gentlemen, and don't expect to be for twenty years; these bars are won only by brevet. I *only graduated this last June from West Point.*'

One of our youngsters, a year or so out of Annapolis, could not understand how a fellow just out of West Point could have seen the service to entitle him to a brevet, and ventured to suggest that he did not know that the class of '66 had any chance in the late war, but was put to utter rout and confusion by the calmly courteous reply, 'You are right, as a class, but three or four of us during cadet furlough went to the front, and I had the further good luck to serve a month on the staff of General Terry, just at the time of Fort

Fisher, and to get a little scratch there that won me these bars.' In fact, he seemed so thoroughly genial, happy, and modestly proud of his rapid advancement, so brimming over with good luck and good spirits, so handsome and natty, that he speedily became the pet of the whole party. When the old admiral came on board he was presented in due form, and that grizzled veteran made even more of him than the youngsters, and so it happened that when our fellows came away they felt that the Frenchmen had far exceeded them in hospitality, in that they could only secure from Captain Dyer a conditional acceptance of their pressing invitation to come and dine with them two days after. 'I cannot promise,' said he, 'because General Terry has received orders to proceed at once to Santa Fé, New Mexico. I am to go with him as aide-de-camp, and I expect orders any minute to join him.'

The next morning half a dozen of us went ashore, among us being a young officer who had a first cousin in the West Point class of '66, and he was particularly desirous of meeting this '*brave jeune capitaine*,' as the Frenchmen called him; and, sure enough, the first uniform we caught sight of as we strolled up toward the Metropolitan (which seemed to be the only hotel in New London just then) was that of Captain Dyer, and I took a good look at him out of sheer curiosity. Why, he looked no older than a boy of seventeen! He was not five feet five in height, but slender as a girl, elegantly shaped, with a smooth, clear-cut, boyish face, large and brilliant eyes, dark, close-cropped hair, and carrying himself straight as an arrow, he was soldierly in every movement. The instant he caught sight of us he had come jauntily forward, with a wave of his delicate kid-gloved hand, and an uplifting of his natty forage-cap, with its gold crossed cannon and silver five. He was dressed in the nattiest possible shell-jacket, then worn by light artillery officers, with the straps of a captain upon the shoulders, and wore dark-blue trousers, with a heavy gold cord, as then worn by staff-officers of the army. Nothing could exceed the frank *bonhommie* of his greeting. He and Preston (as we'll have to call our Annapolis boy who was so eager to meet him) seemed to chum at once. 'What, you a cousin of Will Dixon's! You don't say so! He is one of the noblest fellows in the class, and the happiest days I spent at the Point were those when he and I were room-mates.'

Such were Captain Dyer's words almost verbatim, and, as we strolled along, the two youngsters monopolized the conversation, which was all about West Point and the class of '66, and after a while it occurred to me that it would be a nice day to run out to the fort and see my friend Ford. I left three or four of our party (including Preston), Captain Dyer, and three of the French officers all playing billiards together in the jolliest possible frame of mind.

Ford was not in his quarters. An orderly told me I would find him on the ramparts somewhere, and soon I came upon him, showing the sights to a brace of young gentlemen in civil garb, who were duly presented by him as lieutenants,—I forget their names, but one was of the engineers and the other of Ford's own regiment, the First Artillery. In the course of conversation it transpired that they were on their graduating leave, and that they too were of the West Point class of '66, of which I was beginning to know so much. Ford had known them both as young cadets when he was a first-classman, and it so happened that the engineer had been cadet first captain, and the artilleryman cadet adjutant. Why, I had heard Dyer and Preston talking about them in the most intimate way for the past hour! Their names, as I say, have escaped me after this lapse of years, but as they've got to have names to make the story work, I'll call them Brown and Jones.

Brown, the engineer and ex-first captain, was short, thick-set, squarely built, with a deeply-lined face, full of character and force, a heavy moustache and imperial, while Jones, the artilleryman and ex-adjutant, was, though straight and soldierly, as slender and almost as youthful-looking, and quite as smooth-faced, as the '*brave jeune*' himself.

Thinking to make myself better acquainted, I presently remarked, 'Gentlemen, I had the pleasure of meeting Captain Dyer this morning;' but the announcement seeming to make no impression of the kind anticipated, I added, 'A classmate of yours, I believe.' Messrs. Brown and Jones politely replied that there was probably some mistake. No man of the name of Dyer had been at West Point as a cadet during their time.

'Why! but he's here,' I persisted, somewhat irrrelevantly; 'he's been talking about you both for an hour this morning with Preston, who is a cousin of Dixon's, of your class.'

'Certainly,' said Jones, promptly; 'we know Dixon well. He is one of our most intimate friends.'

'Well,' I continued, 'that's what Dyer says about you. I cannot be mistaken about the name. He says that he lived one year with Mr. Dixon and one year with you, Mr. Jones.'

'I cannot understand it at all,' said Mr. Jones, speaking very courteously; 'the only men of my class who were regularly my room-mates were Brown here, and Smith, of the Fourth Artillery. Did you say General Terry's staff? A captain! Why, Smith *has* a brother with General Terry, but he himself never served with Terry during the war, and wouldn't be masquerading around under the name of Dyer, anyhow.'

I gave them a complete history of the case so far as I knew it. Told them I had seen his name registered at the Metropolitan Hotel, 'Brevet Captain F. Harry Dyer, First Lieutenant Fifth Artillery;' that he had served with General Terry at Fort Fisher, and won his brevet there; that he had had the good luck to be assigned to the Fifth and got his first lieutenancy at once,—to all of which they listened with deep interest and grave politeness, but with evident incredulity.

Unconsciously I found myself growing argumentative in behalf of the hero of my comrades aboard ship. Nothing could have *seemed* straighter than his story. I even went so far as to say, 'Why, Mr. Brown, he said that he had dined with you at your father's house in New Haven, only last week. Isn't your father C. S. A. Brown, of New Haven?'

'Yes,' said Lieutenant Brown; 'but that doesn't help matters. No officer of the army dined with us last week, or for the last month, for that matter, except Jones here, who is visiting me at home.'

This began to look queer. Ford, too, was getting

interested. The youngster *might* be an officer of artillery,—lots of appointments were being made at that time ; but, so far as his statement about West Point was concerned, he *must* be lying, and, *falsus in uno falsus in omnibus*, we four soon concluded to go to town and settle the question.

At the billiard-room we found Preston, who said that Dyer had gone up-town to call on some friends, but would soon return. I at once introduced ' my old friend Ford, of the artillery,' and he in turn presented *his* old friends, Lieutenants Brown and Jones, of the last graduating class. Preston at once recognized the former, whom he had met in company with Dixon some two years previous. 'Why,' said he, ' this *is* luck! I've been talking half the morning with Dyer, of your class. *Won't* he be delighted to find that you and Mr. Jones are here ! '

' Hardly,' said I. ' The fact is, Preston, that's just what I came to see you about. There's something wrong here. These gentlemen say that there was no such man as Dyer in the whole corps of cadets in their time, and that this fellow is an impostor.'

Preston was thunderstruck. He could not believe it; but our plan was soon made.

We took with us a shipmate who happened in at the moment, and who pronounced his inability to believe the young officer a fraud, but was willing to see him put to the test. It was arranged that we should stroll up the main street, and, on meeting Dyer, introduce Lieutenants Brown and Jones as Messrs. Wilson and Tomkins, or something of that sort,—gentlemen from New York,—and let them draw him out.

In ten minutes we met our *soi-disant* lieutenant and aide-de-camp coming toward us jauntily as ever, introduced our civilian friends Wilson and Tomkins, and then, turning, accompanied him back down the street, he walking in front, between his 'classmates,' and Ford, Preston, the gentleman whom I won't name (so don't blush, Ferguson), and myself in rear, where we could overhear the conversation.

It opened briskly. The engineer officer casually remarked that he understood Captain Dyer was a recent graduate, and his tone of voice implied that he looked upon him as a superior being in consequence.

'Yes, sir,' said the victim, with much complaisance of manner; 'I graduated at West Point last June.'

'Did you indeed?' broke in 'Mr. Tomkins.' 'Why, I knew a man who must have been in your class,— Brown, from New Haven.'

'You don't say so!' said the unsuspecting Dyer. 'I'm delighted to meet you then. Brown was one of my warmest friends,—most intimate, in fact. I left him in New Haven last week.'

'Brown was a good deal of a man, wasn't he?' queried 'Mr. Tomkins.'

'Indeed he was! He was our first captain, and a splendid fellow,—one of the best scholars, and decidedly the wittiest man in the class.'

"What sort of a fellow was Jones? He was a classmate too, wasn't he?' asked 'Mr. Wilson,' who, as Brown, must have been no end pleased with so spontaneous a tribute to his worth.

'Jones was a splendid adjutant, a very " military " fellow, as we say at West Point; but he was too conceited to be generally popular, like Brown. Yet I liked him. He was my room-mate a whole year.'

And so it went on. All the way back to the Metropolitan that young fellow discoursed volubly of West Point and West-Pointers, astonishing Brown and Jones with the depth and variety of his information on points they supposed utterly unknown except among the cadets themselves.

Presently we reached the hotel, and there we found assembled a knot of our fellows, who cordially greeted the young captain, and were about to suggest 'having something,' when Ford stepped forward. 'Gentlemen, I beg a moment's indulgence,' said he; 'I have a question to ask Captain Dyer. What battery do you belong to?'

For an instant an ashy pallor shot across the boyish face; he gulped at the attempt to speak, but recovered himself quick as a flash, and stoutly answered, 'I don't know. You see I've never joined,—am even now going on the staff, and have not been assigned.'

'What is the name of your colonel?' asked Ford.

'The colonel—the colonel's name is—is Barnum,' stammered the boy.

'There is no such colonel in the army,' calmly replied Ford.

'And I say there *is!*' loudly and defiantly answered Dyer. 'What do you mean by contradicting me? Gentlemen, who *is* this man?' He turned eagerly, appealingly, to the party of naval officers who stood looking on, petrified with astonishment. For an instant there was a painful stillness. Then Lieutenant Brown, the engineer, stepped forward.

'Look here, youngster! In plain words, you are an impostor. You have represented yourself to be a graduate of the class of '66 at West Point, an intimate friend of Brown and Jones of that class. Now, here we are!— I am Brown, of New Haven, with whom you took dinner last week, and this is your room-mate, Jones. I denounce you as a liar and a fraud, whether you belong to the Fifth Artillery or not!'

Pale as a sheet now, panting with excitement and dread, the little adventurer stuck to his colors,—he made a desperate rally.

'Gentlemen of the navy,' he shouted, 'will you permit this outrage? I am here, your guest, an officer of the army in my uniform, and here I am blackguarded by total strangers. How *dare* you say I am not a West-Pointer? *Who* are you? Where is your uniform? You are a pair of beggarly civilians! How *dare* you affront me? By God, I won't submit to it!'

The scene was certainly dramatic.

Then outspake the gallant tar (Ferguson, *don't* blush, or was it that last glass of claret?). 'Look here, gentlemen, this won't do. Fair play now! Captain Dyer is right, by thunder! Who are you who accuse him?'

'I vouch for the identity of these gentlemen,' said Ford, striding into the group in his artillery uniform, 'and that young scamp is a liar, as they say.' Still the navy party looked dangerously unconvinced, and rallied around their little protégé in a body.

'So do I vouch for them,' said I, 'and so does Preston here. He has known Lieutenant Brown for two years at least.'

'And here is further proof, if you need it,' quoth

Lieutenant Jones, drawing off a heavy seal ring from his finger. 'Here is our class ring. Look at my friend's, it is the same; and there are our names engraved inside.'

The rings were passed around. There was no mistaking them. The castle of the engineers, the shell and flame of the ordnance, the crossed arms of the line, all were wrought of heavy gold, while on the onyx stone was cut the motto, '*Non sibi sed patriæ*,' and within the loop each ring was engraved with its owner's name and the letters ' U. S. M. A., Class of 1866.' But, even now, our *chevalier d'industrie* was not beaten.

'They are frauds!' he cried; 'our class had no ring! We split and decided not to wear it.' Then in came some Frenchmen, and there was more confusion and hubbub; but presently one of our number spoke:

'Gentlemen, this is no easy question to decide. It is a painful business, but each side has its rights. Captain Dyer is under our protection, and shall not be molested.' And with that he turned, and followed by all of the naval representation, except Preston and myself, led Dyer to the door; there the youngster halted.

'I go at once to the telegraph office, to send a dispatch to my uncle, the chief of ordnance—General Dyer —in Washington, and I shall not rest until the police have lodged those two scoundrels in jail.'

So ended the first innings. Messrs. Brown and Jones had only come to New London for the day, and were compelled to return to New Haven by an afternoon train. Twice before they departed, and while still in their company we caught sight of Dyer with a knot of 'blue-jackets,' French and American, around him, and angry glances were cast at our party, but no further collision occurred. Brown and Jones left their addresses with Ford, Preston, and myself, in case anybody had 'anything further to say on the subject,' and went their way.

The next day, when we met aboard ship, the subject of Captain Dyer and the outrage perpetrated upon him by my army friends was *not*, to my surprise, the immediate topic for discussion. In fact, both Preston and myself were struck by the extreme taciturnity of the shore party of the day before. After a while their conduct struck me as suspicious, so I hailed one who had been a prominent spokesman, and asked—

'What answer did your *protégé* receive to his dispatch to General Dyer?'

'Don't know,' was the somewhat gruff reply, as the gentleman turned impatiently away. So I accosted another with a cheery ' Well, Mr. ——, did you dine with Captain Dyer last evening?' The only reply was a glare of wrath. This was becoming mysterious; so, presently, Preston and I tackled a third member of the party with ' Look here, F——, what's got into you all this morning? Have you found that little rascal out at last?'

F—— turned upon us suspiciously. 'Haven't you heard?' he asked; and when we swore we hadn't, he explained, reluctantly.

'Well,—he jumped the town last evening, d—n him! and left his bills behind.'

A week afterward, in the *Army and Navy Journal*, under the head of Personals, we read a notice something like this: 'Brevet Captain F. Harry Dyer, First Lieutenant Fifth Artillery, left the city yesterday, *en route* for

Santa Fé, New Mexico, where he is to join the staff of General Terry;' and a week after that came another to this effect: 'A correspondent has called our attention to the fact that there is no such officer as Brevet Captain Dyer, First Lieutenant Fifth Artillery, in the army; and, after reading his letter, we are prompt to confess ourselves the victims of an impostor. We received and published the notice in all good faith, not thinking it possible that any trickery was intended.'

Next we got a letter (at least Preston did) from Lieutenant Brown. In a few words he told us that he had traced Dyer's antecedents completely. ' He was a very smart boy who, some years before, had so interested a wealthy resident of New Haven that the latter sent him to Russell's Military School, supplied him with money, and meant to educate and bring him up as his own. The youngster had taken a notion that he would like to go to West Point, and so," wrote Brown, " he came to my father and told him he had an appointment, and my father encouraged him to come to the house or his office, talked to him by the hour of myself and classmates, which accounts for so much that he knew. Now it seems that a large number of petty thefts at the school, that had been going on for months, were traced to him a month ago, and he cleared out, and, last of all, it has just been discovered that he has forged his benefactor's name for several hundred dollars.'

So much for Captain Dyer. Any time, for a year after that, that you wanted to get half a dozen fellows on the *Winnebago, fighting mad,* you had only to mention that name. Ferguson, your face to-night reminds me vividly of an inflamed countenance I once saw away back in '66.

Now, this isn't a Christmas story so far, I admit. These are only prefatory remarks, however. We'll come to Christmas presently. You see, as I warned you at the outset, I have no practice as a talker, and so, once started, my tongue runs away with me.

Of Captain Dyer nothing more, to my knowledge, was ever heard; but, in the course of the next few years, the *Army and Navy Journal* contained frequent allusion to a mysterious character who turned up unexpectedly, like an inland Flying Dutchman, in all manner of places where the junior officers and midshipmen of the navy had relatives; invariably to the financial detriment of those warmhearted people. For months the columns of the journal were graced with sketches of the flying visits paid by this erratic party, who was described to be young, graceful, handsome, stylishly dressed, ordinarily in undress naval uniform, particularly easy and winning in his manners, and invariably out of cash and in need of a temporary loan.

What father could refuse it to the intimate friend of his boy at sea? What mother did not eagerly listen to his stories of their laughable adventures, or bless him for his touching recital of some instance of her boy's nobleheartedness? Time and again we read of his swindling somebody or other, and one night Preston, looking up from his paper, accosted a chatting group with 'I say, you fellows! what do you want to bet this "Bilged Midshipman," as they call him, isn't your old New London acquaintance, the *brave jeune capitaine?*'

Well, Christmas holidays of '68 had come; and, with a short leave, I had run out to Detroit to visit some relatives and army friends then living there. Gay times they were having that winter. The city was full of pretty girls. Parties, dances, balls, and dinners were crowding upon one another. A regiment of infantry and a light battery, quartered at Fort Wayne, and a dozen engineer officers in town, made the item of beaux an easy one. I fell into the music naturally enough, though I only got there three days before Christmas, and was having the thoroughly delightful time that, in my opinion, a fellow of either service only has in its full perfection in that hospitable 'City of the Straits.' The army men know it ten times better than we do, but I never yet saw a man in the navy who didn't want to get back to Detroit,— once having paid it a visit.

On Christmas morning, as we were coming out of church, I was suddenly seized upon by one of the most genial and charming ladies in society. Old enough to be the mother of one of our most dashing young ensigns (which accounts for her seizing upon me), but so young and kindly in her disposition as to be the favorite of all the young people in society.

'Oh, Mr. Ratchet!' she exclaimed, 'we only heard of your arrival last night, and my husband went down to call upon you the first thing this morning, but you had left the hotel. Now, *don't* tell me you are engaged for Christmas-dinner or I shall be in despair. Now that my Jack is away in the Pacific Squadron, I have no comfort so great as meeting his friends. You *will* dine with us, won't you? We have quite a little party of pretty girls and army men, but I do want one more of my boy's friends with us. Mr. Walton is the only one, and he'll be so rejoiced to see you.'

'Walton?' said I. 'What Walton?' forgetting for an instant the invitation.

'Why, George Walton. Jack's classmate at Annapolis. He said that you were marine officer on the *Winnebago* with them in '66, but he had no idea you were in this part of the country.'

'No more had I that he was here,' answered I, and with that we strolled off down Jefferson Avenue together, chatting about Jack and his voyages and comrades. I had accepted her invitation gladly enough, for I knew that my bachelor friends would excuse me. The avenue was crowded with people walking blithely homewards in the keen frosty air, and with brilliant sleighs dashing to and fro to the music of their merry bells. Suddenly Mrs. Britton exclaimed, 'There's Mr. Britton now,—and our sleigh,—and Mr. Walton!'

I glanced quickly as the sleigh darted by, but only in time to catch a fleeting glance of the occupants. I saw Mr. Britton's jovial face and silvery hair, and by his side a handsome young fellow jauntily raising a navy undress cap from his shapely head. Not Mr. Walton by a good deal, as I remembered him, but— where the mischief had I seen that face before?

No chance was given me to ask further questions. Mrs. Britton was joined by friends, to whom I was presented; and when we parted at her door I had only time to ask where Mr. Walton was staying. Ten minutes after I was overhauling the register of the Russell House, and there, among the arrivals for the 23d, was the name George Walton, U. S. N. He had gone sleigh-riding with Mr. Britton, said the clerk; but would I leave my card? No, I wouldn't leave my card, but would wait. I *did* wait,—something like two hours, it seemed to me, staring out at the snow-covered street, feverishly reading the newspapers, and keeping vigorous watch all the time for the return of this Mr. Walton. The genuine possessor of the name and rank I believed to be far away in the China seas. Now, who was the handsome youngster I had seen in Britton's sleigh? The face haunted me.

But, after all, my watch had to be broken. An engagement took me up-town again, and then I had just time to dress and hurry to the Brittons.

A bright party of young people were there assembled, and chatting away with far more jollity than is usually the case when waiting for dinner.

But where was Walton? Every now and then Mr. Britton would fidget and look at his watch. 'I wonder what keeps Mr. Walton?' he said. 'We are only waiting for him.' A quarter of an hour passed, and the missing guest came not. A messenger was sent to the hotel, and meantime dinner was announced. We were discussing turkey and the inconstancy of sailors in general, when the messenger returned, and handed Mr. Britton a note, which, with an apology, he opened and read. 'Bless my soul!' he exclaimed, 'what can this mean?' and then read aloud,—

'RUSSELL HOUSE,
'Dec. 25, 6.45 P. M.

'MY DEAR SIR,—Mr. George Walton, U. S. N., took his valise and left the house immediately after returning from his drive with you. He left no word as to his destination. (Signed) BRIGGS, C'lk.'

I could hold in no longer. 'Will you pardon me for a very impertinent question, Mr. Britton? I have earnest reasons for asking if Mr. Walton made any mention to you of being in need of a little pecuniary assistance?'

'Why,' said our host, reddening and stammering, 'it is a matter I'd rather not speak of. I—I—in fact, *cannot.*'

'You need not fear harming George Walton's good name, sir. You have simply been victimized by the "Bilged Midshipman." I met him in '66 as 'Captain Dyer.'"

By the time that the marine officer had finished his story the commanding officer was evidently becoming uneasy, and at once broke in with the remark that it was very late for ship hours, and that he feared he must excuse himself.

"Oh, Tangent," said the admiral laughingly, "the old ship won't run away from you, and Christmas only comes once a year."

"Well, admiral," said the captain, "before we separate I am glad of the opportunity of calling upon my old messmate, the paymaster, for his own 'Saturday Night' song, as appropriate to-night as on the last evening of the week. Some few of us are old enough to remember another song—addressed to a member of your corps, by the way, paymaster, which was as good a thing of the kind as ever was written,—

'Here's a health to thee, Tom Breese,
Tom Breese of the bounding billow!'"

But Mr. Balance's lines seem to me to come nearer to our hearts than even that. "Tom Breese" was an *outward-bound* song, while this is a real *homeward-bounder*. And I know, too, that for some reason the paymaster has never sung it during this cruise, and therefore the probability is that no one present, except myself, has ever heard it.

In a moment (to the surprise of every one but the captain) the paymaster, in a mellow, but rather overripe tenor, began the following verses:

> Come, messmates, fill the cup once more;
>   We'll drink, before we part,
> The toast that long has sacred been
>   To every sailor's heart.
>
> The toast that's passed our trembling lips
>   On many a distant shore,
> And sounded in our loyal hearts
>   Above the ocean's roar.
>
> The toast that all the gallant dead
>   And all the living brave,
> That sleep beneath the ocean's breast
>   Or float upon its wave,
>
> Have pledged so oft with faltering voice,
>   And with a glistening eye,
> On many and many a distant sea,
>   'Neath many a foreign sky.
>
> The toast that bears our spirits back
>   On memory's wings to-night,
> To homes where loved ones, clustering
>   Around the firesides bright,
>
> With gentle voices murmur
>   Fondly of those who roam;
> Where little ones are lisping,
>   "When will papa come home?"
>
> Where wives beloved and loving,
>   And maidens pure and fair,
> To-night our names are breathing
>   In earnest, holy prayer.

And not a doubt is whispered
Of those so far away;
They ask not God to keep us true,
But for our safety pray.

Then drink the toast, it cheers our hearts,
And lightens all our cares;
It mingles with our daily thoughts,
And with our nightly prayers.

Mid calm or storm, on land or sea,
Whenever we may roam,
With heart and lip we'll pledge the toast,
" Sweethearts and wives at home."

For some time before Mr. Balance ceased his song the ship's motion had been felt to change, and ominous sounds of incoming studding-sails and of " working ship" had come faintly down the hatch, causing the captain to fidget a little, and the admiral to glance at the beams for a tell-tale compass, which was not there.

These sounds, and the change of motion, would, probably, not have attracted the attention of a landsman seated at the table, and yet every soul there present knew what they meant.

Just then appeared a midshipman to say, " Captain Tangent, the officer of the deck reports that the wind has come out ahead, and ship's head is off to south-sou'west."

" Very good, Mr. Butt!" said the captain, in a cool and perfunctory tone and manner; and then, rising, he said, " Gentlemen, we've lost the Trades early, and this is the last pleasant weather we shall have," and up on deck he went without another word.

" Good-night, gentlemen!" said the admiral. " I

thank you for a pleasant dinner. We've a long pull yet before us, and more than one northeast snow-storm, and northwester to follow, before you see your sweethearts and wives."

And they were both right!

There's No Doubt

about the curative effects of *Scott's Emulsion* of Pure Norwegian Cod Liver Oil and Hypophosphites of Lime and Soda in the first stages of consumption. Dr. Koch's Lymph treatment is still on trial, but *Scott's Emulsion* has been tried so effectually and so frequently as to be past experiment.

Scott's Emulsion cures Coughs, Colds, Consumption, Scrofula, General Debility, and all Anaemic and Wasting Diseases. It prevents wasting in children. *It is palatable as milk.* Scott's Emulsion is put up in salmon-colored wrappers. *Be sure you get the genuine.* It is prepared only by Scott and Bowne, New York, and sold by all Druggists.

Scott's Emulsion

A happy thought, that, to print a whole story in each number of a magazine; not a short story, either, but a full-fledged novel, such as magazines used to take a year to complete. Only a wide-awake magazine would have thought of it. It *was* a wide-awake one,—LIPPINCOTT's. And such stories!

The new idea came in with a whoop with a story of Habberton, entitled "Brueton's Bayou." 'Twas setting a high mark for whoever followed. There was no question about the Bayou, but what of what was to come?

Well, they've been coming once a month ever since for *sixty months.* Up to the mark! Plump! Crowd the mark, if anything. And there are many more to follow. It is not only the novel that you get, but a good magazine, besides. Chock full of bright articles on popular subjects, poems, sketches, short stories, and lots of other things. Is it a wonder the circulation *jumps?* It pays to be wide-awake.

Single numbers, 25 cents. $3.00 per year.

Address
LIPPINCOTT'S MAGAZINE,
PHILADELPHIA.

Van Houten's

"Samivel, my boy, they've a quar-relled. Yer mother-in-law says there's nothin' like Van Houten's Cocoa, an' the shepherd sticks to his rum and water. There's no need to drop him in the water butt after all, Samivel"

Tony Weller.

Cocoa.

"Best & Goes Farthest."

The Standard Cocoa of the World.
A Substitute for Tea & Coffee.
Better for the Nerves.

At all Grocers. Ask for VAN HOUTEN'S. Purity unquestioned—"Once tried, always used."

☞ It only needs a single trial to convince any one of the superiority of VAN HOUTEN'S COCOA. Please insist upon VAN HOUTEN'S *and take no substitute*. It is put up in **1-8, 1-4, 1-2** and **1 lb.** Cans. ☞ If not obtainable, enclose 25c. in stamps or postal note to either VAN HOUTEN & ZOON, 106 Reade Street, New York, or 45 Wabash Ave., Chicago, and a sample can will be mailed postpaid, *if you mention this publication.* Prepared only by VAN HOUTEN & ZOON, Weesp, Holland.

The Philadelphia Record

THE
LEADING MORNING NEWSPAPER
OF PHILADELPHIA.

CIRCULATION, 140,000.

A Complete Newspaper with all the Attractive Features of a First-class Magazine.

SUBSCRIPTION RATES.
(POSTAGE PREPAID.)

Daily, without Sunday, One Year $3.00
Daily, including Sunday, One Year 4.00

For Advertising Rates, address

The Record Publishing Company,
917-919 Chestnut Street,
PHILADELPHIA.

MILITARY NOVELS BY CAPT. CHARLES KING, U.S.A.

CAPTAIN BLAKE.
With Illustrations. 12mo. Cloth, $1.25.

"It is like a long draught of clear, cool spring water after a hot and dusty desert ride to read this fresh, breezy, wholesome story, peopled by manly men and womanly women, and full of the bold, free life of the soldier on the frontier, with enough of the schemes of scamps to give it lively interest, and abounding in brilliant and charming pictures of the life of the soldier in the quiet of peace at the remote frontier posts and the thrilling excitement of battle with wily, savage, and desperate foes. . . . Captain King has done much to give the people at large, who have known next to nothing of the dangers and privations and priceless services of our small military force, a better idea of what the country owes to its meagre but gallant force of defenders. He writes of the life, the dangers, the joys, the sorrows, of which he has personal knowledge, and there is no more lagging or dulness in this tale than in many of the wonderful marches made by the force of which he is a worthy member. This story is one of his best."—*Chicago Times.*

THE COLONEL'S DAUGHTER. With Illustrations	$1.25
MARION'S FAITH. With Illustrations	1.25
STARLIGHT RANCH, and Other Stories	1.00
KITTY'S CONQUEST	1.00
LARAMIE; OR, THE QUEEN OF BEDLAM	1.00
THE DESERTER, and FROM THE RANKS	1.00
TWO SOLDIERS, and DUNRAVEN RANCH	1.00

"He is a graceful and vigorous writer. His novels are sure to be out of the common run: he depicts military life on the frontier with a fidelity that has won much praise; his romance is always pure and sweet; and while he is sometimes severe with his women characters, he has the art of setting forth the better qualities of the sex with enticing realism. In a word, he is simple and natural in all that he writes. To take up a book from his pen is to be sure of an hour of harmless pleasure."—*Boston Beacon.*

For sale by all Booksellers. Sent by the Publishers, post-paid, on receipt of the price. J. B. Lippincott Company, 715 and 717 Market Street, Philadelphia.

| CATHOLICS | IN THE
U. S. ARMY and NAVY

desirous of reading a first-class Catholic newspaper, are requested to send for a specimen copy of the

CATHOLIC STANDARD

before subscribing for any other.

Ably edited in all its Departments, and uncompromising in its advocacy of Catholic principles, the STANDARD is one of the best—if not THE best Catholic newspaper published in the United States.

Subscription, $2.50 Per Annum, in Advance.

ADDRESS
HARDY & MAHONY,
PUBLISHERS AND PROPRIETORS,

☞ P. O. BOX 1044.   PHILADELPHIA.

GRAND NATIONAL PRIZE OF 16,600 FRANCS.

CONTAINING

Peruvian Bark, Iron
AND
Pure Catalan Wine.

Endorsed by the Medical Faculty of Paris, and used with entire success for the cure of

MALARIA,
INDIGESTION,
FEVER and AGUE.
NEURALGIA,
LOSS of APPETITE,
POORNESS of BLOOD,
WASTING DISEASES,
and
RETARDED
CONVALESCENCE.

An experience of 25 years in experimental analysis, together with the valuable aid extended by the Academy of Medicine in Paris, has enabled M. Laroche to extract the entire active properties of Peruvian Bark (a result not before attained), and to concentrate them in an elixir, which possessed in the highest degree its restorative and invigorating qualities, free from the disagreeable bitterness of ordinary preparations.

This invigorating tonic is powerful in its effect, is easily administered, assimilates thoroughly and quickly with the gastric juices, without deranging the action of the stomach. Iron and Cinchona are the most powerful weapons employed in the art of curing; Iron is the principle of our blood, and forms its force and richness. Cinchona affords life to the organs and activity to their functions.

E. FOUGERA & CO., Agents, No. 30 North William street, New York. 22 rue Drouot, Paris.

FOUNDED 1839.

Jas. B. Rodgers Printing Co

Nos. 52 and 54 North Sixth St.

Philadelphia, Pa.

Book and Catalogue Printing,

———— ALSO

Commercial Printing

Electrotyping.

Coughs and Colds.

For Throat Troubles and Lung Affections of whatever character, Dr. Jayne's Expectorant is a rational, safe and successful curative.

The Cough which accompanies a simple cold may inflame and rack the Lungs until serious pulmonary trouble is engendered. This Expectorant will subdue any tendency to inflammation and radically cure the Cough. In Sore Throat or any Bronchial Disorder, it will remove the feverishness of the parts and cleanse and heal the lining membrane of the throat. It will overcome the cause of Asthma and afford prompt relief. In Consumption, small doses will ameliorate most of the symptoms, and especially relieve the Cough, remove Soreness of the Lungs, and promote their healing. In Croup and Whooping-Cough, it is most helpful, checking the violence of the attacks and relieving the attending distress.

It is a good Remedy for

Pleurisy,	Difficulty of Breathing,	Coughs of all kinds,
Spitting of Blood,	Inflamed Lungs,	Throat Ails,
Pains in the Breast,	Hoarseness,	Congested Lungs,
	Asthmatic Affections.	

It Heals the Lungs.

The Churchman
ESTABLISHED 1844.

Subscription, in advance, $3.50.

The Leading, Largest, most Widely Circulated Weekly in the Episcopal Church.
It gives over 2500 pages annually.
It commands the Highest Subscription Price of any Religious Weekly in America.
Its Constituency is the Wealthiest.
Its Circulation is, in consequence, the Choicest.
It is the only Illustrated Denominational Weekly.
It is the Handsomest Typographically.
Its Magazine Form promotes its Preservation.

STATISTICS OF THE
PROTESTANT EPISCOPAL CHURCH,
OCTOBER 1, 1890.

Clergy	4,200
Parishes	3,500
Communicants	508,500

More than five-eighths of whom, or over 300,000, are in the New England and Middle States.

The exceptional wealth and liberality of this religious body is shown by its contributions for Church purposes for one year of

$12,720,000, or over $25.00 each communicant,

nearly one-half more than the Presbyterian (North), which with 775,900 members contributed to January 6, 1890, $14,368,131, or nearly $19.00 each; one-half more than the Congregational, which with 491,985 members contributed to May 1, 1890, $8,444,999, or nearly $18.00 each; and two and a half times more than the Methodist Episcopal, which with 2,236,463 members and probationers contributed to October 1, 1890, $21,000,000, or nearly $10.00 each.

THE CHURCH YEAR, Jacksonville, Florida, the only Episcopal Weekly published south of Richmond, was consolidated with **THE CHURCHMAN** January 31, 1891.

M. H. MALLORY & CO.,
47 Lafayette Place, New York, N. Y.

"TRITON"

BRAND OF PLAYING CARDS

---- ARE ----

"SQUEEZERS"

Our Cards are used by the leading Clubs and Army and Navy. All dealers have them.

SAMPLE PACK MAILED ON RECEIPT OF 25 CENTS.

Be sure you see the word **TRITON** on the box and wrapper of each pack. Ask for **TRITONS**; they are double enameled.

We also make the No. 35 Hart's Squeezers, and over 25 other grades of cards.

N. Y. CONSOLIDATED CARD CO.

W. 14th Street, New York.

BY LAND AND SEA.
Edited by Capt. CHARLES KING.

A collection of short stories of Military and Naval adventure, written by officers of the Army and Navy. Among the contributors are:

Capt. CHAS. KING, U.S.A.	Capt. H. D. SMITH, U.S.R.M.
Capt. EDWARD FIELD, U.S.A.	Mr. E. L. KEYES, late U.S.A.
Lieut. T. H. STEVENS, U.S.N.	Capt. WM. C. BARTLETT, U.S.A.
Lieut. F. S. BASSETT, U.S.N.	Lieut. JOHN P. WISSER, U.S.A.
Capt. HENRY ROMEYN, U.S.A.	

and several other officers, including one of high rank in the navy, whose names will be announced in due time. The book will be a companion volume to the "Colonel's Christmas Dinner," although somewhat larger in size than that book, and the price will be 50 cents a copy, postage free.

The stories are all new, and written expressly for this book.

THE COLONEL'S CHRISTMAS DINNER.
Edited by Capt. CHAS. KING, U.S.A.
PAPER, 200 PAGES.   12mo.   PRICE, 50 CENTS.
LIST OF CONTRIBUTORS:

Introduction	By Capt. CHAS. KING, U.S.A.
The Adjutant's Story	" Capt. CHAS. KING, U.S.A.
The Senior Lieutenant's Story . .	" Lieut. THOS. H. WILSON, U.S.A.
The Senior Captain's Story . . .	" Capt. EDWARD FIELD, U.S.A.
The Junior Captain's Story, . . .	" Capt. HENRY ROMEYN, U.S.A.
The Colonel's Daughter's Story, .	" Miss CAROLINE F. LITTLE.
A Captain's Story, ...	" Capt. W. C. BARTLETT, U.S.A.
The Quartermaster's Story . . .	" Mr. EDWARD L. KEYES.
The Major's Story, ...	" Major. WM. H. POWELL, U.S.A.
A Guest's Story, ...	" ALICE KING LIVINGSTON.
The Colonel's Story, ...	" Col. H. W. CLOSSON, U.S.A.

These stories are all of military adventure. They are supposed to be told over the walnuts and the wine at a dinner given by the Colonel of the regiment.

The publishers venture the assertion that no book of the kind, published here or abroad, excels in literary merit or exceeds in typographical beauty this dainty volume.

The picture on the title-page was drawn for us by **Mr. T. S. Sullivant.**

TRIALS OF A STAFF-OFFICER.
By Captain CHARLES KING, U.S.A.

This volume is composed of the sketches Captain King has contributed at intervals during the past five years to the UNITED SERVICE. It contains

"THE ADJUTANT."   "THE ORDNANCE OFFICER."
"AT WEST POINT."
"THE TELEPHONE AS AN ADJUNCT TO THE NATIONAL GUARD."
"MILITIA INSPECTIONS."
"MILITIA CAMPS OF INSTRUCTION."   "SHAM BATTLES."
"THE ADVANTAGES OF ONE'S OWN WORKSHOP."
"HOW WE ELECTED THE MAYOR OF OGLETHORPE."

These sketches are written in Captain King's happiest vein, and one critic has pronounced them the best literary work the author has ever done.

The book is handsomely issued in paper, 200 pages, 12mo., at 50 cents, and will be sent by mail, postage paid, at this price.

L. R. HAMERSLY & CO., Publishers, 1510 Chestnut St., Philada.

THE THREE VOLUMES WILL BE SENT FREE OF POSTAGE FOR $1.00.

Safest, Fastest, and Finest Trains in America,

RUN VIA

Baltimore and Ohio Railroad

BETWEEN

NEW YORK, PHILADELPHIA, BALTIMORE, and WASHINGTON.

All trains vestibuled from end to end, and protected by Pullman's Anti-Telescoping Appliance, including Baggage Cars, Day Coaches, Parlor Cars, and Sleepers. All Cars heated by Steam, and lighted by Pintsch Gas. Pullman Dining Cars attached to famous five-hour trains between New York and Washington.

THE BALTIMORE AND OHIO RAILROAD

Maintains a Complete Service of Vestibuled Express Trains between

NEW YORK,

CINCINNATI,

ST. LOUIS,

and CHICAGO,

EQUIPPED WITH

PULLMAN PALACE SLEEPING CARS

Running through without change.

ALL B. AND O. TRAINS

BETWEEN THE

East and West,

RUN VIA WASHINGTON.

PRINCIPAL OFFICES:

211 Washington Street, Boston, Mass.	1351 Pennsylvania Av., Washington, D.C.
415 Broadway, New York.	Corner Wood St. and Fifth Ave., Pittsburg, Pa.
N. E. Cor. 9th and Chestnut Sts., Philadelphia, Pa.	Corner 4th and Vine Sts., Cincinnati, O.
Cor. Baltimore and Calvert Sts., Baltimore, Md.	193 Clark Street, Chicago, Ill.
	105 North Broadway, St. Louis, Mo.

J. T. ODELL, General Manager. } BALTIMORE, MD. { CHAS. O. SCULL, General Passenger Agent.

Earles' Galleries
816 Chestnut Street, Philadelphia, Pa.

Facsimiles
Etchings
Proof Engravings
Water Colors
Oil Paintings
Mirrors
French Miniature Frames
Tasteful Picture Frames

For home Decoration and Bridal Gifts

DOBBINS'
ELECTRIC SOAP

Is for sale everywhere, and has been ever since 1869.
Acknowledged by all to be

THE BEST FAMILY SOAP IN THE WORLD.

We ask every woman using it, to save the OUTSIDE WRAPPERS and send them to us. We will mail her, postpaid, the following Beautiful Presents, gratis:

For each Twenty-five complete outside wrappers, a lovely panel picture, "La Petite," by a foreign artist, superior to our "Two Sisters" or "L'Hiver" for beauty and artistic merit.

For each Twenty complete outside wrappers, any volume of the "Surprise Series" of twenty-five-cent novels. Nearly 200 volumes, and about 200 pages each.

If preferred, two wrappers and ten cents in stamps or cash may be sent instead of twenty wrappers, for these books only.
Send one cent for catalogue of novels.
Very best Authors.

For each Sixty complete outside wrappers, we will mail a Worcester Pocket Dictionary, 298 pages.

To those who prefer to assist Religious or Charitable Institutions we make the following offer: Instead of sending the above presents, we will pay cash at the rate of fifty cents for each 100 *complete outside* wrappers sent us. It makes no difference whether they are sent us direct by the lady using the Soap, or saved, and given by her to her favorite institution, *no matter what denomination*, and by them sent to us. We will send the money to the person sending us the wrappers. This will give needed financial assistance to worthy charities, at no expense to you. We propose to donate thus, at least one hundred thousand dollars a year. Among hundreds of worthy institutions are all the Little Sisters of the Poor, Orphan Asylums, Sisters of Charity, Hospitals, Women's Relief Corps, G. A. R. or S. of V. Soldiers' Homes, W. C. T. U., "King's Daughters" Circles, etc.

I. L. CRAGIN & CO.,
Manufacturers Dobbins' Electric Soap,

No. 119 S. Fourth Street, Philadelphia, Pa.

 Should the Penn Mutual Life Insurance Company pay the publishers of this volume for the privilege of occupying this space? Why should it advertise at all?

IT HAS OVER EIGHTEEN MILLION DOLLARS OF ASSETS.

Its clear surplus over all liabilities, present or future, is nearly **Two and a half Million Dollars.**
In 1891 it received for premiums and interest, $5,001,508.34.
It paid to Widows and Orphans, and to living members, $2,312,042.97.
It applied to reserve, so as to make absolutely certain the payment of all other contracts as they mature, $1,682,907.
It wrote $25,600,000 of new insurance.
It pushed the total of Insurance in force to $104,000,000.
Quite a little responsibility, to be sure!

It doesn't need business—don't have to have it, and won't accept it unless it comes on such terms as will promote the prosperity of every member of the corporation.

It advertises that **YOU** may participate in its benefits, and it invites you to become a member solely because an extension of its business may come to mean a reduced cost to all. A merchant knows that he can sell a million dollars' worth of goods at a less ratio of expense than a half million.

——ADDRESS——

The Penn Mutual Life Insurance Co.,
921, 923, and 925 CHESTNUT STREET,
PHILADELPHIA.

www.ingramcontent.com/pod-product-compliance
Lightning Source LLC
Chambersburg PA
CBHW020922230426
43666CB00008B/1536